Support Services and Mainstream Schools

A Guide for Working Together

Edited by
Mike Blamires and John Moore
in association with NAAOSEN at the Centre for Enabling Learning,
Canterbury Christ Church University College

 David Fulton Publishers

David Fulton Publishers Ltd
The Chiswick Centre, 414 Chiswick High Road, London W4 5TF

www.fultonpublishers.co.uk

First published in Great Britain in 2004 by David Fulton Publishers

10 9 8 7 6 5 4 3 2 1

Note: The right of the authors to be identified as the authors of this work has been asserted by them in accordance with the Copyright, Designs and Patents Act 1988.

David Fulton Publishers is a division of Granada Learning Limited, part of Granada plc.

Copyright © The individual contributors 2004

British Library Cataloguing in Publication Data
A catalogue record for this book is available from the British Library

ISBN 1 84312 063 1

Typeset by BookEns Ltd
Printed and bound in Great Britain by Thanet Press

Contents

Acknowledgement

The editors would like to thank the contributors to this book. They would also like to thank their own families for their consideration and support, in particular Joanna Blamires for her proofreading of the chapters.

Preface

This book is the result of a collaborative venture between the National Association of Advisory Officers for Special Educational Needs (NAAOSEN) and Canterbury Christ Church University College.

The National Association of Advisory Officers for Special Educational Needs is an association for LEA and independent advisers/consultants and LEA officers concerned with special educational needs. Members share information through a BECTa mail list and conference facility in the Virtual Teacher's Centre site. The Association aims to provide mutual support through the exchange of news, ideas and documents. It also provides a voice for officers and advisers working in special educational needs, including those working in the wider field of additional educational needs.

The subject of support services and their future is one of considerable interest to NAAOSEN members, who are often required to advise LEAs on appropriate development, and, increasingly, in the light of greater delegation to schools, to play a direct role in managing services retained by the local authority.

The contributions to this book reflect the range of local authority advisory officers and private consultants that make up the membership of NAAOSEN.

The issues discussed in this book, therefore, arise from current practice and the desire to ensure the best possible service to early years settings and schools in their endeavour to include a wider range of children and young people with additional educational needs.

The relationship between NAAOSEN and Canterbury Christ Church University College is long-standing. The Centre for Enabling Learning, within the Department for Professional Development and the Faculty of Education at Christ Church, has a national research profile in relation to issues of inclusion, disability, difficulty and difference, alongside an extensive professional development programme. Members of NAAOSEN have contributed both to research and professional development activities of the centre.

Contributors

Robin Attfield, National College of School Leadership
Mike Blamires, Canterbury Christ Church University College
Ann Butt, Derby Unitary Authority
Claire Cosser, Derby Unitary Authority
Gill Dixon, Warwickshire LEA
Naresh Gahir, Warwickshire LEA
Peter Gray, independent educational consultant
Gill Henderson, Shropshire LEA
John Moore, Kent LEA
Kevin Mulryne, Warwickshire LEA
David Prior, independent educational consultant
Marion Russell, Lancashire LEA
Christine Salter, London Borough of Bexley
Linda Samson, Kent LEA
Rob Skelton, Nottinghamshire LEA
Maggie Stephenson, Kent LEA
David Teece, Warwickshire LEA

Support services: growth and development

Robin Attfield, Mike Blamires, Peter Gray and John Moore

Introduction

If schools and early years settings are to be successful in enabling the social participation and academic achievement of all children and young people within their communities, they will need to look beyond the boundaries of their own expertise and experience, and demonstrate a willingness to work with others who have the appropriate knowledge, skills and understanding. Traditional support services alone, however, whether statutory agency or volunteer-based, can no longer claim to have the monopoly of being a single point of reference and must now adapt to being part of a dynamic, flexible and evolving resource which may include the local community, special and other schools, regional organisations, national charities, local trusts and parents' groups. For this expertise to have impact, however, the school will have to ensure wide acceptance and ownership of in-school systems that are capable of assimilating or accommodating this expertise. This has not always been the case, and in order to consider where support services are going we must first consider where they have come from, and what, for them, constitutes development.

Remediation

Support services effectively began with the introduction of education psychology services in 1913 and the appointment of Cyril Burt by London Council as the first educational psychologist. The purpose was to allocate children to the limited number of special school places, this being 2 per cent of the school population, assuming a 'bell curve' distribution of intelligence. The work of Burt has continued to exert influence despite the considerable criticism that exists about the validity of his research and the deficit nature of educational need it supports. It is reflected, for example, in the DfES SEN Programme of

Action (1998) that sets 2 per cent of the school population as the target for the provision of a Statement of Special Educational Needs. Whatever the criticism, however, Burt's work paved the way for clinic-based casework in most LEAs.

Later, the 1944 Education Act made clear the responsibility of LEAs for making provision for pupils for whom 'special educational treatment' was required (this excluded those then deemed ineducable, who came into the educational system following the 1970 Education Act). This led to additional training opportunities in a number of fields and the development of specialisation in teaching methods that were different from those applicable to most pupils. By the time of the Warnock Report (1978), the integration of some groups of pupils with additional educational needs was becoming established and specialist teachers were more involved in mainstream work, particularly in relation to sensory impairment and reading skills acquisition.

Much of the development from this point on, as noted by the Warnock Report, took the form of peripatetic teaching for children with a range of difficulties. This usually involved the withdrawal of pupils for individual or small-group lessons, with the aim of remediation in literacy skills. These lessons took place in local centres or, if in schools, outside the classroom. The HMI report of 1989 noted that the accommodation for these lessons was often of a poor quality, making use of corridors, school halls and medical rooms. The derogatory term for such accommodation soon became known as 'the broom cupboard'. The growth of support services from this time has been well documented and readers are advised to turn to Gipps *et al.* (1987), Dessent (1987); and Moses *et al.* (1988) for further analysis.

Advice and differentiation

After Warnock, the intended role and language of the support services changed. The work was to be 'advisory' rather than 'remedial', with a focus on supporting class teachers responding to their pupils with special educational needs. This exhortation for change, however, did not always translate into practice. Duffield *et al.* (1995) investigated the beliefs and working practices among support teachers in Scotland using the key aspects of the support role as suggested by the Scottish Committee for staff development. The support teachers listed them in order of importance as follows:

Aspect of role	Rated as 'of prime importance'
Co-operative teaching	44
Consultancy	23
Individual teaching	20
Staff development	<4

So while the rhetoric had been 'out of the cupboard and into the class and across the school', the support teachers themselves were reluctant to extend their impact much beyond the classroom. In the late 1980s the focus changed from 'meeting special educational needs' to ensuring access to common curriculum entitlement. In 1989 the National Curriculum Council published *A Curriculum for All* (NCC 1989) which,

> By emphasising the role that ordinary teachers could play in identifying and meeting the special educational needs of pupils, the guidance effectively carried forward the view that good practice in teaching such pupils was no different from providing effective learning experiences for pupils generally. Much of the rhetoric prior to 1993 (The Education Act and subsequent Code of Practice) was concerned with mechanisms for sharing expertise, for demystifying special education practice and for enskilling ordinary class and subject teachers to 'own' the professional issues by enabling them to acquire enlarged repertoires of pedagogical strategies. (Evans and Docking 1998: 50)

As a result it was thought that learners with special educational needs did not need to be taught different things from their peers or to be 'remediated'; they needed to be taught the same things as their peers but in different ways. The task for support teams was therefore to support the development of 'appropriate' differentiation in teaching and learning. The focus moved from special provision to 'appropriate' teaching in the context of a common curriculum delivered in a variety of ways and in response to a diversity of learners. Such a change in emphasis, if adopted whole-heartedly by a support service, might have brought a further challenge to their credibility, as they had to be seen as 'super differentiators'.

Advice versus support

As services developed during this period, there were lively debates about the appropriate balance between 'advice' and 'support' and the legitimacy of those giving advice without an appropriate range of teaching experience. More fundamentally, there were those such as Dessent (1987) who contended that the continuing presence of extensive external support services potentially 'deskilled' mainstream schools and prevented them from developing their own more inclusive responses to pupils with special educational needs. Moore and Morrison (1988), however, suggested that support services had a key, if transitory, role to play in schools accepting responsibility for all pupils.

Statutory assessment

Interestingly, while support services generally expanded throughout the 1980s, their work became increasingly linked to the statutory assessment process. This appeared to be for two main reasons: first, LEAs began to look to support services for advice about pupils' eligibility for additional resourcing (as demand for statutory assessments started to escalate). Secondly, services found themselves playing an increasing role in managing and overseeing the work of a range of additional teaching and non-teaching staff who were allocated to individual pupils with a Statement of SEN.

In this respect, while the philosophy of many services still espoused a significant role in mainstream school development, in practice, the focus of much of their work remained with individual pupils. There were, however, developments in the degree to which support services worked 'in context', with assessment and support happening more often in the classroom rather than on the more traditional withdrawal basis.

Delegation

At the same time, however, the growth of support services slowed and their range of activity across LEAs became more diverse due to the impact of delegated budgets to schools under the Local Management of Schools (LMS) initiative. The Education Reform Act (1998) brought in requirements for LMS under the assumption that local education authorities had been bureaucratic, wasteful and misdirected in their use of funds to support schools (Lee 1992, cited by Marsh in Clough 1998). The assumption of LMS was that schools, by themselves, knew 'what was good for them'. Prior to this, schools were funded on the basis of:

> (a) historic funding – where schools were given allocations because that was what they were allocated;
> (b) officer allocation – an LEA officer decided upon allocation, possibly taking into account judgements of where needs were greatest; and
> (c) bidding – where schools bid for extra funding for prescribed projects or needs.
> (Knight 1993)

There was an expectation that schools should be funded directly to provide for most of their pupils' needs. In some LEAs, this meant some existing support service funds being immediately transferred to school budgets. In others, transfer of funds happened more progressively as they were increasingly delegated, particularly for some support service areas (Bangs 1993; Evans and

Lunt 1992). The extent of delegation was increasingly affected by the need to match government-funded targets and, in some LEAs, to avoid mainstream school budget reductions.

Government guidance began to distinguish between elements of LEA service provision that were 'mandatory' and those that could be retained centrally as 'discretionary exceptions'. This had a significant impact on the balance of different support service areas, with a tendency to retain services such as Educational Psychology, Sensory Impairment Teams and support for statemented pupils, and to delegate or reduce other areas of support that only had discretionary status.

Other limiting factors included the historic levels of provision for mainstream and special schools, the amount of funding required for centrally retained services such as educational psychology and educational social work, the availability and cost of service-level agreements as well as the influence of pressure groups. Furthermore, the introduction of Grant Maintained Status for some schools meant that such schools would be directly funded, thus further reducing the amount of money available to LEAs.

Thus the shift in balance of power between LEAs and schools led to a greater emphasis on the school as purchaser of LEA services, with a greater tendency for services to evaluate their contribution in the school's terms. This prompted a number of commentators (e.g. Bowers 1991) to speculate whether support services would ultimately work on a 'freestanding' basis, selling services more directly to schools and others.

School responsibility and market forces

The more explicit separation of school and LEA funding raised issues about the appropriate balance of responsibility for providing for pupils with special educational needs. LMS required the majority of funds to be distributed directly to schools. The 1981 Education Act, however, placed statutory duties on LEAs to ensure that appropriate provision was made for pupils with SEN, particularly those whose needs were 'significantly greater or otherwise different from' other pupils of a similar age. Continuing uncertainty about this area and growing pressure for statutory assessments in many LEAs led to various reviews (Audit Commission 1992a and b; House of Commons Education Committee 1993) and, ultimately, to the SEN Code of Practice in 1994. This was expected to provide a clear point of reference for both schools and LEAs about their respective responsibilities. In addition, it offered a framework for the involvement of SEN support services, working preventatively with schools at stages 1–2, engaging more actively with individual pupils at stage 3 and playing a part in the LEA's statutory assessment and provision process at stages 4–5.

The greater emphasis on school responsibilities for stages 1–3 of the Code tended to validate an emerging view in a number of LEAs that funding for these stages should be delegated, with resources retained to support LEAs' more clearly identified statutory responsibilities. Most LEAs, however, continued to see a need for support services to play a moderating or 'gatekeeping' function, even though the Code of Practice had attempted to articulate clearer criteria by which appropriate stages of assessment could be judged (Fletcher-Campbell 1996). In fact, the association in many LEAs between Code of Practice stages and SEN resourcing made the need for some form of external moderation increasingly necessary.

Some services reacted speedily and offered services in the marketplace. In contrast to early expectations, delegation of SEN support services at stages 1–3 was not typically accompanied by 'buyback' arrangements (where schools use delegated funds to purchase LEA support service time). During the second half of the 1990s, therefore, it was not uncommon for the more preventative elements of LEA service to be lost.

A legacy in some areas was that expertise built up over time became dissipated as schools chose to make their provision autonomously, often in the form of additional teaching assistance. This pattern was particularly apparent at the secondary level, perhaps for three main reasons:

1. economies of scale made such organisation worthwhile;
2. an SEN department existed to build and oversee such development; and
3. high schools have been more accustomed to working in this way.

This did not necessarily mean that overall support service capacity reduced. In a number of LEAs the decline in preventative aspects was more than matched by growth in levels of support provision for statemented pupils. Furthermore, emerging concerns in schools and LEAs about pupils with emotional and behavioural difficulties (linked to the rise during this period in the number of permanent exclusions, Parsons 1997) led to increases in behaviour support provision, either in terms of mainstream support capacity (Gray *et al.* 1994) or provision in off-site units (Pupil Referral Units (PRUs)). This was assisted by increases in government funding for local authority projects linked to truancy and disaffection.

In addition, there was some development in the number of specialist posts, linked to specific areas of LEA concern (e.g. autism; dyslexia). These appeared to relate in part to areas that were proving to be contentious in the context of parental appeals to the newly formed SEN tribunals (Gross 1996). With this increased autonomy of schools, LEA support services could only be delivered if the schools opted to use some of their budgets to buy services from the LEA rather than an alternative provider. This resulted in an uneven pattern of support which, alongside a change in focus, it could be argued, led to the Audit Commission reporting on three occasions (1992a, b and 2002) that learners with special educational needs without Statements were sometimes poorly served by mainstream schools.

Standards and inclusion

As mentioned above, some of these concerns also led to the Special Educational Needs Code of Practice in 1994, and to its revision in 2002, to which all schools must 'pay due regard', and also the government's revision of the SEN programme of action (DfES 2003a). The impact of league tables, however, has meant that schools have continued to be competitive, and as purchaser of services they have exerted a strong influence over the form of support they wish to receive.

Schools, therefore, are not only under pressure to improve standards but also to respond to a wider range of learning needs. Recent guidance from the DfES (2001b) on inclusive schooling and from Ofsted (2001) on the inspection of inclusion, alongside the SEN and Disability Discrimination Act (2001), require schools to be accountable for their practice in meeting the needs of both under-achieving groups and pupils identified as having special educational needs. While schools have gained more responsibility in this area through delegated funding, however, local support services have steadily diminished, thus arguably reducing the capacity of schools to respond.

The Audit Commission Report (2002) suggests that LEAs review their approach to providing support as part of a more fundamental and wide-ranging review of how they provide services to meet special educational needs. In the light of the above, two key questions may be asked concerning the balance of delegation to retained service and what strategic role the LEA envisages for support services. The two are closely linked, and many of the chapters in this book illustrate how LEAs and services have worked to bring clarity of direction to the support service function in relation to the dual, if often competing, demands of promoting inclusion and improving standards.

Questions to be addressed

The issues that characterise the response are addressed here through practical examples dealing with a variety of pupil needs. Some of the more important questions these examples raise are as follows:

How can schools organise themselves to make best use of services offered?
How can services work together to ensure that the most vulnerable groups achieve?
How can support agencies work together to promote support for particularly difficult groups such as those with mental health needs whom often 'disappear' between the services of two agencies?
How can support services improve the process of transition between phases of education?
Is support to an individual school the most effective way of working or can more be achieved through working with a community of schools?
What happens when you delegate all your resources to schools, and can a service operate in a business culture?
What is the best balance of funding as regards delegation and retained services?
How do we know this is the best way to work?
Is there such a thing as effective evaluation for services, and what is best practice?
How can special schools make a meaningful contribution to the promotion of inclusion through outreach and support?

   In approaching these questions, the editors have developed a simple audit tool (Chapter 2) which places each key feature within a developmental framework. We have used the metaphor of the 'broom cupboard' to describe early beginnings. Teachers, formally located within centres, on becoming peripatetic, often found themselves teaching individual children away from the classroom setting, sometimes in less than satisfactory surroundings. The development of each feature is then traced through phases of transition represented by working in the classroom, working with the whole school and, ultimately, working in the broader community of schools. The latter, echoing to some degree the government's SEN Programme of Action, concerned with 'inclusive education systems'.
   Although we have used the term 'best practice' to describe the final transition to the wider community, it is understood that many support services will be at different points along the continuum. There may be good reason for this, not least that services can only evolve and innovate as fast as schools allow,

supported by a clear strategic brief from their authority. Table 2.1, therefore, sets out the features along this continuum and the intention is that services use the matrix as a means of identifying their next zone of development. This can then be coupled with the evaluation procedures outlined in Chapter 13 to plan a way forward that moves them towards best practice. In setting out the features against transition phases we have posed six critical questions:

- What is the service trying to achieve?
- What are the competing agendas between the service, other services, the school and the LEA? How will these be resolved or negotiated?
- Who is actually doing the supporting and how are they doing it?
- Who has the expertise and how is it applied?
- What is the balance and focus of the main functions?
- How well are we evaluating what we do?

These themes are developed in the final chapter, building on the examples contained in the chapters that follow.

Conclusion

Finally, this book makes the case for a new way of working between support services and schools that will reap the benefits of prior experience, specialist knowledge and expertise within support services and enable them to perform a strategic role in developing inclusive practice. It makes use of the extensive knowledge and experience of advisers, support services and advisory services concerned with meeting special and additional educational needs. Its objective is to share examples of good practice with those using and developing services for schools and to increase the achievement and inclusion of learners with diverse needs.

2

Asking the right questions: a development model

Mike Blamires and John Moore

Reflecting on the issues outlined in Chapter 1, Table 2.1 sets out the key stages of development of a support service, from early involvement with individual pupils outside the classroom to the more advanced state of working in an integrated fashion with other services and agencies across a 'community' of schools. It addresses the six questions raised at the end of that chapter by setting out 'indicators' of practice for the key features of service development that these questions imply, namely: vision, agenda, initiative, mode of operation, ownership of experience, central tasks, relationships and evaluation of impact.

What is the service trying to achieve?

By 'short-term expediency' we mean a lack of vision of how schools might develop self-sufficiency in meeting all their pupils' needs. As many of the case studies in the following chapters demonstrate, in the longer term services must see themselves as part of a more global approach to education, as described by Samson and Stephenson (Chapter 10), where schools and services collaborate to achieve this end. Many recent government initiatives recognise the power of schools working together: Excellence Clusters; the Leadership Incentive Grant; and Confederated Governance. All have the same basic appeal – that of sharing strengths and expertise. If this can work for underperforming secondary schools, it can also work for schools that need to become more inclusive.

Underdeveloped services, however, may be some way from taking advantage of these initiatives. Some will only be at the point of integrating the pupil and therefore support will be at the level of the classroom. Others will have moved on to whole-school planning for longer-term effect, by ensuring that their work is represented in the School Improvement Plan. Typically, the least developed will be reactive, organising themselves to respond to crises that occur when

Table 2.1 Key Stages of Development of a Support Service

Question	Main Feature	Cupboard — Least developed practice	Classroom → Transition	Whole-School → Transition	Community → Best practice
What is the service trying to achieve?	Vision	Short-term expediency Reactive Responding to crises	Integration of pupil and support work into the classroom	Longer term planning of support through School Improvement Plan Proactive problem-solving	Working for an inclusive culture in a community of schools. Towards self-sufficiency in meeting all pupils' needs
What are the competing agendas between the service, other services, the school and the LEA? How will these be resolved or negotiated?	Agenda Initiative	Service agenda oriented Little contact with other services Encouraging support dependency Operates from own expertise base Reactive single service team	Service and Teacher Responding to teacher and pupil need Inter-disciplinary collaboration Negotiating agenda	Service and SENCO Challenging policy and practice across the school Inter-disciplinary planning meetings	Service and school(s) Collaboration Clear and understood protocols Enabling inclusion in the context of school improvement Proactive The ability to relate quickly to agencies and others Focused team which includes schools
Who is actually doing the supporting and how are they doing it?	Mode of operation	Encouraging dependency Treatment culture	Prescriptive packages of support and intervention	Teacher ownership Well-researched and strong theoretical base for interventions	Enhanced capacity for inclusion through school development Specialist teaching Development of a focus supporting school improvement and single pupil service plans
Who has the expertise and how are these applied?	Ownership of expertise	Guarding expertise and importing expertise into schools Individual pupil support focus	Sharing expertise with class teacher Supporting curriculum change	Support to whole-school policy development and practice Sharing expertise across the school	Expertise shared across agencies and groups of schools Priorities turned into projects Giving away expertise
What is the balance and focus of the main functions?	Central Tasks	Isolated Diagnostic Assessment Responding to severity of pupil need	Assessment to monitor individual pupil progress Responding to teacher's planning	Assessment to diagnose school development needs Responding to whole-school development needs	Cross-agency assessment and planning Project orientation
How well are we evaluating what we do?	Evaluation of Impact Relationship	No clear method for evaluating effectiveness	Teacher/parent satisfaction as evaluation	School satisfaction with service	Agreed, clear mechanisms for evaluating current position shared across schools and agencies

schools fail to solve problems from within their own resources. At first glance this may appear to be consistent with School Action Plus of the SEN Code of Practice, but reactive services rarely find themselves in a partnership of problem-solving. It is more likely that they will be viewed as the 'expert' when all else fails. Unfortunately, when they fail, which in some circumstances they must (see Chapter 3), schools may more readily place the blame on the service, with a subsequent loss of credibility. Proactive services work with schools to prevent crises, and at its best this is achieved with other agencies on a planned basis across schools willing to share their resources and expertise, as described in Chapter 4.

What are the competing agendas between the service, other services, the school and the LEA? How will these be resolved or negotiated?

There will be few services that recognise themselves as being substantially in the column of 'least developed practice'. Having moved 'out of the broom cupboard' and into the classroom they will have embraced curriculum change; the culture of target-setting and the change in balance of control brought about by delegation and local management. Indeed, it will not have been possible to retain former working practices, given the enormous pressures on schools to improve performance. The introduction of national strategies for literacy and numeracy, first in primary schools and now at Key Stage 3, and the complex often conflicting agendas of social inclusion and national target-setting, demand a different approach where teachers are supported to make sense of these difficult tasks. This requires those providing the support to give consideration to teacher planning at class and year group level. Add to this substantial changes in SEN and disability legislation and statutory guidance, and it is not difficult to see why there has been a significant shift not only from the cupboard to the classroom, but from direct teaching to advice.

This changing agenda, however, has brought the additional challenge of the school defining its own support needs. This is most acute where LEAs have moved towards a cluster arrangement for schools where head teacher 'boards' or elected management groups consider the appropriate allocation of LEA retained resources in relation to the cluster's perceived priorities. Needless to say, these priorities may differ considerably from those of the service. In addition, there will be pressures from other agencies, particularly where the 'children's service' agenda has gained momentum. Services will be used to working with different multiagency plans such as the Early Years Development and Childcare Plan

(EYDCP), but will be less used to direct negotiation on such issues as the medical basis of behaviour and the most effective deployment of therapies. Effective support will require this level of detailed agreement if schools are to make the most of integrated working across services and between groups of schools.

If schools are to be supported to be more inclusive, therefore, the development of support services will need to go much further. The range of needs within any one school or group of schools will be such that services will not be able to operate in isolation. This is by no means an easy process as was recognised as far back as 1981:

> However desirable interdisciplinary working may be, it is not achieved simply by sitting people from different backgrounds down together. Means must be found of enabling professionals to communicate with each other and to do so at a professional level, avoiding the two extremes of using language and concepts not accessible to colleagues and resorting to common-sense exchanges... Though the latter may be useful in limited ways it is not interdisciplinary working. That requires that the people involved act as professionals contributing something that is specific to their professional background but which is also accessible to other professionals. This would seem to be more difficult than is commonly supposed.
>
> (Hegarty *et al.* 1981: 204)

The problem, however, persists. In a more recent discussion of these issues led by Tony Dessent at the London Institute of Education (NASEN SEN Policy, Options, Dessent 1996), Seamus Hegarty, Director of the NFER, was observed to pour scorn on interdisciplinary activity at the level of strategic management and commissioning, forcefully making the case for a determined focus on day-to-day encounters between professionals in the field. In truth, both levels are required if support services are to stand a chance of moving forward together.

This difficulty is also highlighted by Lacey (2001) who notes that Leathard's (1994) review of research into interprofessional work found over 50 terms which are used to denote different forms of professional work.

Orelove and Sobsey (1991) suggest three conceptualisations of working among agencies, which have important ramifications for services that are summarised below:

Multidisciplinary – with professionals from more that one discipline working alongside, but separately from, each other so that there may be duplication alongside fragmentation with the potential for complementary outcomes left to chance. Such an approach often arises from silo funding and targets.

Interdisciplinary – refers to the sharing of information with jointly agreed action between disciplines, but each input is delivered discreetly by members of the separate programmes.

Transdisciplinary – 'is held to be the most developed model of working which involves sharing or transferring information and skills across traditional boundaries to enable one or two team members to be the primary workers who are supported by others working as consultants'. In Lacey and Lomas' (1993) version of this, emphasis is placed on the role of the key worker who embodies this role as part of a small team of co-workers delivering different, but complementary, aspects of the programme.

Lacey's research on interprofessional work within a special school found that, while the literature praises increased co-operation and collaboration between disciplines, in practice a good deal of anxiety and even hostility is created.

It is perhaps useful to refer to the definitions of these two terms within the psychology of personal constructs (Kelly 1955). Anxiety is defined as the awareness of an individual that she may not have the skills, knowledge or understanding required to deal with a forthcoming event or challenge, while hostility is the active refusal to adapt to the implications of forthcoming events or challenges.

As is well demonstrated in the chapters that follow, the issues raised by the above continue to pose a significant challenge, but the service of the future will need to find a way of working within the context of both inter- or trans-disciplinary working and inter- or trans-school collaboration. There must be one team, perhaps representing many professional functions, but working as one service. Such teams could indeed be drawn from a number of services but could act as a single team in respect of the group of schools they serve. This team will be inclusive of expertise within the client schools and be broad enough to encompass services offered by special schools and 'resourced' mainstream schools. The outcome for the parent, pupil, the school or group of schools could be one unified support plan.

The team will have clear and understood protocols of operation and be focused on enabling schools to develop the skills, policies and cultures required for improving inclusion, in the context of school improvement. It will plan on a project basis, with clear mechanisms for agreeing priorities with schools and providing monitoring and evaluation strategies to track progress and to demonstrate impact. It will have the ability to relate quickly to non-statutory agencies and voluntary groups. It will know how it arrived at what it is going to do, know when it has achieved this and to what effect, and be clear that this represents best value.

Who is doing the supporting and how are they doing it?

Services at an early stage of development will guard their expertise and be somewhat precious about professional status. This often leads to a culture of importing expertise into schools, resulting in defensiveness when methods are challenged. To ensure that this does not happen such services will often develop a strong dependency relationship with teachers, either through removing the child for 'treatment' or through the production of highly prescriptive packages that depend on the expertise of the support agent for implementation. These packages change with fashion and tend to disable mainstream teachers with the associated jargon. They can enhance the status of the support service member, as they have a product to offer and another string to their bow. These packages, however, can have their own theoretical basis, disembodied from established knowledge derived from evaluation and research. At their worst they may threaten the confidence and competence of teachers to respond to the needs of their learners. Some are supported by partisan claims for efficacy, often with a select group of learners in a setting that may be difficult or inappropriate to create in the mainstream. Accompanying the package will be training required for authorised usage. Rather than being an extension or change in emphasis of existing teaching, these packages tend to be bolted on to the practice of the school. For this reason they will have a precarious foothold on mainstream practice. Where packages are well researched with a strong theoretical base relevant to classroom practice; then the approaches they promote may have a positive influence. The key to success, however, is ownership by the teacher.

In this context, 'tips for teachers' may have a part to play in supporting high-quality teaching and learning but teachers need to be aware of the danger of using methods and materials that do not readily integrate into their own skills repertoire. Confident support empowers teachers to develop a skill, which in turn reduces dependency and enhances competence and confidence in responding to diversity (Thomas 1992).

A useful distinction between 'specialist teachers' and 'specialist teaching' has been made by the Teacher Training Agency in their document on Specialist SEN Standards (1999) which attempts to establish a framework for schools and services to audit their professional development needs.

Lindsey (2000: 46) suggests that

> the development of professional expertise ... derives from a large number of experiences with children with a variety of Special Educational Needs, which both informs the professional with the range of issues, and the probability of differential effectiveness of intervention. This enables such specialists to respond more competently, quickly and effectively when faced with a child whose needs are not easily understood.

Such expertise may be difficult to come by for mainstream teachers, especially in relation to low-incidence needs, and support services can work with mainstream teachers to develop specialist teaching.

Applying existing knowledge and strategies across similar and contrasting settings is a further dimension of expertise to be developed. Lindsey also suggests that 'schools cannot always audit skills and knowledge alone – they don't know what they don't know'. Schools are not alone; they share many similar competing agendas, challenges and experiences and can benefit from strategic planning and sharing of resources. Support Services are in a unique position to enable this.

Who has expertise and how is it applied?

The agenda of increasing inclusion and participation (SNAP DfES 2003a; DfES 2001a; QCA Inclusion Statement 2000) across education implies that schools should become more adept in providing successful educational opportunities for an increasing diversity of learners. It has been contested in some quarters (e.g. Ainscow 1999; Billington 2002) whether new skills, knowledge or understanding need to be applied in order to respond to diversity. In addition, the means of locating or developing such expertise has also been challenged. Ainscow has stated that all that is needed for inclusion is a will and commitment and that the school has very often the resources it needs to include all its learners. Hart (1997) also suggests that difficulties in learning can support a process of reflection in which barriers to learning for all learners can be examined and overcome. Alternatively, mainstream practitioners have questioned the practicality of exhortations for parochial problem-solving, where the wheel has to be repeatedly re-invented with little or no reference to the experience of others. Where time is at a premium the process of discovery, learning and reflection appear to be neither efficient nor effective and a greater emphasis on networking and consultation is called for.

Tomlinson (1982) and, more recently, Billington (2002), on the other hand, have suggested that support services are not only irrelevant but also actively conspire in the removal of learners from the mainstream.

Dessent (1987), as referred to in Chapter 1, has suggested that the role of support is even more counterproductive when external support services deskill mainstream schools, preventing them from developing their inclusive responses.

Such criticisms have been part of the development of a social model of difference and difficulty which continues to challenge the authority of professionals to make decisions concerning the inclusion or exclusion of individuals considered to have 'special educational needs'. Support services need, therefore, to be seen to be in the business of enhancing the professional expertise of teachers through the continuous development of their specialist teaching skills that are shared across different schools.

What is the balance and focus of the main functions?

In a recent review conducted by a large LEA, it was found that a significant proportion of all service time, including those provided by health (some 60 to 70 per cent), was taken up by monitoring progress through assessment. Teachers felt that substantially more time could have been given to establishing viable intervention programmes, working alongside the teacher. Perhaps given the limited time available to most services, this is an unrealistic expectation, but it does demonstrate significant variation in perception between schools and services as to what their respective roles should be. It also demonstrates that services within this LEA are some distance from applying expertise in the manner outlined in the above section.

In our matrix we have suggested the need to move away from such 'isolated' diagnostic assessment and review, with its accompanying focus on the severity of individual pupil need, towards more project-focused activity. This activity focused on working with the school and other agencies to develop a school-based capacity for pupil assessment, review and intervention. This is particularly important if the practice of 'intervention' is to be part of the inclusive culture of the school.

Further, service activity is to a large extent dictated by the nature of the assessment and diagnosis it undertakes. Most services have moved on from isolated pupil diagnostic assessment but, as can be seen from the example above, many remain at the level of periodic review of pupil progress. Diagnostic assessment and review is not necessarily inappropriate and may well be needed for some pupils. In isolation, however, it does not help the teacher or school to work with the child in the context of the overall learning opportunities created by the school (e.g. see Butt and Cosser Chapter 7 and Dixon and Gahir Chapter 8).

Tasks can of course be multilayered, and we are not suggesting that services abandon working directly with pupils or cease diagnostic work; only that this should be followed through at the level of the teacher's planning and whole-school development needs. Projects which involve other partners and a spread of expertise seem to us to be the most likely way of managing these multilayered activities efficiently. The assessments and reviews are more likely to be effective if the suggested interventions are part of an inter- or trans-disciplinary team approach, where the interventions recognise and utilise expertise within the school and have direct significance for what the school is attempting to do for all its pupils.

Furthermore, the enhanced status of the Special Needs Co-ordinator in mainstream schools, resulting from the SEN Code of Practice, consequent legislation and guidance, has meant that schools are more aware of the gaps in their special needs provision. They have a clearer idea of what they need and who may be able to help. They have, therefore, become more critical consumers of support services. The process of school self-review directed at increasing the school's capacity for inclusion will be informed and enhanced by drawing upon the expertise of several disciplines, made easier by the use of a project-based approach.

Since this is a partnership between the service and the school it can be expected that the school will contribute to the performance review of the service.

Beek (2002), cited in the Audit Commission handbook for LEAs on special educational needs, suggests a framework for considering the interrelationship between schools and LEAs in respect of monitoring and accountability. Here the LEA provides 'challenges' that schools build into their development planning as part of their capacity building. In Chapter 14 we consider how support services might contribute to this challenge through school improvement activity.

How well are we evaluating what we do?

> Success of support teams should not always be measured only by pupil progress. Schools may require both direct and indirect support and general guidance. Evaluation should take account of any role in increasing schools' capacities for managing pupils with SEN. (Audit Commission 1992b para. 86: 55)

It could be argued, however, that the agenda dictated by league table indicators has diminished the importance of measuring and reporting on the progress of learners with special educational needs. What counts for meeting special educational needs might not be included within the existing accountability frameworks. Whether this will be put right by more inclusive value-added measures remains to be seen. The audit commission has noted this point more recently:

> In contrast to the national standards of attainment, little is known about the outcomes achieved by children with SEN. A lack of monitoring of their achievement and a lack of relevant performance measures make it difficult to

recognise the good work in many schools, or to identify where children are poorly served.

Schools feel pulled in opposite directions by pressures to achieve ever-better academic results and become more inclusive. National performance tables and targets fail to reflect the achievement of many children with SEN. Government needs to find a way of recognising and celebrating the achievements of these pupils and their teachers, often against considerable odds.

(Audit Commission 2002: 41)

The report goes on to state that barely half of LEAs have systems for monitoring work on SEN in mainstream schools. Of the 66 respondents, 22 were monitoring school expenditure, 24 were monitoring the effectiveness of school management on SEN and 20 were monitoring the outcomes achieved by pupils with SEN.

At school level the HMI report, in 1996, found that 'the majority of governing bodies take only a limited lead and leave the school staff to make their own decisions'. Governors are frequently unsure about circular 6/94: 'The Organisation of Special Educational Needs', which offered guidance on provision. They were also unsure about what constituted success criteria or how they should report on the allocation of resources to meet special educational needs. Schools also failed to supply nominated special educational needs governors.

Services have had to address these issues by reviewing and adapting the range of guidance and support offered to schools and establishing new criteria to measure effectiveness.

As the role of support services develops, the challenge to effective self-review becomes greater. The progress from cupboard to classroom to school and community brings with it a requirement to monitor the quality of the interplay of a range of relationships, but ultimately, as the Audit Commission points out, the effectiveness of any service will be judged upon two sets of criteria: pupil progress and the increased capacity of schools for inclusion. In other words, how well support brings together the two agendas of standards and inclusion.

A service or a group of services cannot evaluate their impact, however, outside of a more systematic approach to monitoring, challenge and intervention led by the local authority. Our experience suggests that LEAs are at different starting points in their evaluation of service effectiveness, depending on the context. All of the following, for example, influence the service's ability to both provide effective support and evaluate impact:

Spending on SEN varies from £2 million to £105 million – and ranges from 10 per cent to 23 per cent of spending on schools;

LEAs delegate between 40 per cent and 80 per cent of their SEN budget;

the proportion of children with statements varies from less than 1 per cent in some LEAs to more than 4 per cent in others; and

the proportion of children educated in special schools varies from less than 0.2 per cent to more than 2 per cent.   (Audit Commission 2002)

This variation in policy, provision, resourcing and needs profile of the population will all influence priorities for action and provide an important backdrop for the evaluation of services. It is important, therefore, that there is a shared understanding of the LEA's starting point.

If we accept the Audit Commission's (2002) view that there are three key challenges facing LEAs in the management of SEN, namely establishing a sound strategic base; developing the capacity of schools and early years settings; and monitoring, challenge and intervention, then evaluation will need to address all three in relation to the working of services. In particular, it will need to address the support service role in school monitoring and self-review.

Conclusion

In the first two chapters of this book we have endeavoured to demonstrate that services to support additional education needs in mainstream schools and early years settings stand at a crossroads. The gap in the pace of change in schools, and services in particular, brought about by new initiatives, will make it difficult for services to respond in a way that is supportive to an agenda of increasing inclusion. For some the gap may be too great for them to survive. Others will, however, as the following chapters demonstrate, strengthen their role through innovative work, meeting the challenge of change by forging local partnerships of services and schools to reap the benefits of prior experience, specialist knowledge and expertise.

This is the vision. There will be many roads to achieving it, and many obstacles along the way. The contributors to this book demonstrate practice that will move services towards this goal.

3

Additional support: improving inclusive practice in mainstream schools

Robin Attfield

Editors' introduction

In this chapter Robin Attfield draws on a range of contrasting case studies to show different stages of development within mainstream schools for working with support services. Attfield emphasises the role of the Special Educational Needs Co-ordinator in ensuring that the school is capable of harnessing and taking ownership of the expertise on offer. He suggests some common features of schools that promote inclusion and stresses that support for schools is as important as support for individuals and that measures of value-added should take into account social outcomes as well as academic results. Attfield discusses the importance of leadership in developing a shared ownership of inclusion across the school, rather than 'seclusion' where responsibility for 'special educational needs' remains with the SENCO and teaching assistants.

What are the ideal conditions? What are the barriers?

Effective inclusion requires a number of conditions to be in place. These will vary in relative importance according to context (historical, geographical, environmental, financial and educational). The writer is concerned, however, that, nationally, there is no agreed definition of inclusion. While accepting fully that inclusion is a process (DfEE 1997), and recognising the value of the QCA (2000) advice on its curricular aspects, this lack of clarity will foster differing interpretations. This not only impacts on practice but also on evaluation. For the purpose of this chapter, inclusion is seen as creating the environment for inclusive learning for all pupils. Successful inclusion will focus on all of the students' learning, not just those elements defined as 'academic'.

Some features of an effective environment for inclusion are:

- leadership commitment to high standards for all;
- staff commitment to meeting the needs of all pupils;
- commitment to teamwork;
- commitment to ongoing staff learning;
- commitment to improvement;
- teaching, and especially learning, at the heart of the school;
- declared policy of commitment to all pupils which informs practice;
- diversity is not only accepted but celebrated;
- staff knowledge;
- high expectations of all pupils.

In the words of a nursery head, considering the implications of educating a blind pupil for the first time, 'if we wait for every factor to be in place before we start working, the pupil's time with us will have come and gone'. Her commitment was to make as many anticipatory arrangements as possible and work in a reflective manner with other stakeholders, seeking to provide the most appropriate arrangements as all became more fully aware of the child's needs.

For inclusion to take place schools may need additional staffing and/or expertise beyond that which is normally available. The provision of additional support, however, will produce its own dilemmas. Mainstream settings that are able to include all pupils with SEN without additional support are rare. Where the school is willing to work with others, however, to enhance knowledge and skills, alongside the ability to work in a genuine partnership, most obstacles can be overcome. These barriers and solutions to them are explored through the case study scenarios described below.

Scenario 1 – purpose

In a high school, additional resourced provision was made for pupils with moderate to profound hearing impairment. The philosophy of the provision was for pupils and staff to be fully included. The specialist teaching staff taught mainstream subjects (including to examination level) and undertook other roles and duties in line with mainstream colleagues. Each pupil followed an individual timetable of mainstream lessons, with additional support provided through tutorials to prepare for, or to follow up lessons. There was close involvement with mainstream staff and materials to support schemes of work had been prepared. In-class support was provided only infrequently. Pupils spent between 40 per cent and 100 per cent of their time in mainstream lessons.

Tutorial time was available outside school hours on a regular basis. In Years 10 and 11, some courses to examination level were provided entirely within the resourced provision, as access to conventional course delivery was limited. Occasionally, alternative courses were provided. It was common practice for most pupils to take one less subject to give time for tutorial work.

At one stage, there were two girls with very similar backgrounds and hearing losses. In discussing arrangements with the girls for their Y10 and Y11 programme, it was agreed that one (Mary) would follow a complete range of mainstream subjects but that the other (Jenny) would only follow two mainstream subjects (one with reduced examination requirements and additional practical/social aspects) within the resourced provision. Parents and mainstream staff were happy with the arrangements. Within the resourced provision, Jenny was in a small group for one subject but was taught individually for the other. This did not mean, however, that she had undivided attention from a specialist teacher as there were other pupils present from other years on other courses.

Both pupils' progress was reviewed regularly and was at least satisfactory. When examination results were published in the Summer of Y11, Jenny's results were better than Mary's. When her lesser academic ability was taken into account, the difference was significant. This raised a number of questions. Was the quality of teaching suitable and was there sufficient support for the pupil fully included? Had the additional attention given the less academic pupil the confidence to overachieve? Would more flexible mainstream grouping have offered more opportunity for targeted in-class support?

In discussion, all parties, including mainstream staff, parents and pupils, felt pleased with the outcomes for both pupils. In particular, Mary's self-confidence was noted; her very good social relations with peers and the development of a group of friends outside school time. (The school was not the neighbourhood school and was a bus ride away for both girls.) Both did well post-sixteen, but Jenny remained significantly less socially competent than Mary and was far more dependent upon her family as a young woman.

Commentary

The case study highlights a number of issues relevant to inclusion in the current context. A number of strengths are apparent within the scenario described. Joint decision-making and pupil involvement were good. There was flexibility of provision. Both pupils made good academic progress against their prior attainment. However, in a world of accountability, exam results alone would suggest that one pupil succeeded significantly more than the other. Yet this measure fails to take into account the wider and less tangible aspects of social competence and self-esteem. In terms of preparation for wider life, was one pupil over–supported? Would she have done as well academically if placed in mainstream courses and would she have been better served for her future? Appropriate professional judgements were made for and with the pupils and these were based on clear views about pupil needs. Academic results alone give an incomplete picture and there is an urgent need to include a balanced view of pupil achievement. What is worrying in the wider context is the different emphasis given to the importance of inclusion as a criterion for success between schools and support services reported in the study by Gray (2001).

Scenario 2 – partnership

Within a newly established support service, consideration was given to a menu of possibilities for the role of the support teacher. Support was allocated to schools not only through statements but also for non-statemented need. Approaches were broadly agreed in a 'contract' between school and service managers, but precise working arrangements were agreed at teacher level.

In a primary school, where support work was agreed by all parties to be particularly effective, the support teacher worked from a menu of possibilities. The involvement was for four hours weekly with two hours allocated to a particular class where a number of pupils were undergoing formal assessment and the rest allocated to early intervention within Key Stage 1. Intervention included:

- team teaching within the KS2 class, in which the support teacher worked intensively with a group of pupils but also led whole-class work on a weekly basis to allow the class teacher time to work with pupils with SEN;
- regular work with nominated pupils in KS1 on intensive programmes in the 'catch-up' mode;
- supporting school assessment with the SENCO;
- developing support materials with nominated subject teachers;
- case conference and review attendance; and
- planning liaison with class teachers, usually before school.

An external evaluation of the school praised the use of differentiated materials, which not only made the curriculum more accessible for those with special educational needs but also supported the acquisition of basic literacy skills across the curriculum.

Commentary

There was discussion in the school about how best to use the support available, and this was negotiated from a suggested menu. Practice developed over time, with mainstream staff becoming increasingly aware of the role support could play and the impact it could make. A balance was struck between intensive small-group and wider support, and the pupils did not see support as primarily targeted to nominated individuals but as an additional resource for the class. Above all, the support was viewed as positively enabling the school to meet the needs of all of its pupils.

Support teachers can work in a variety of ways and it may be appropriate for the specialist to work intensively with pupils for part of their time. What the above demonstrates, however, is that mainstream staff who receive no support as a result of this targeted work to individuals can view nominated pupils as the responsibility of others, and may be resentful of the specialist working in this setting.

Scenario 3 – inclusion or seclusion

Scenario 3 encapsulates visits to two mainstream schools where Teaching Assistants were employed as part of provision for meeting pupils' special educational needs. All TAs in the high school were employed directly, whereas in the primary school, the element for statemented pupils was held centrally, with the TA operating from a special school base.

In the primary school, there were two TAs. One had worked exclusively with a pupil with a physical disability and associated learning difficulties for a number of years. The pupil was nearing the end of KS2. The other TA worked in-class in KS1 for some time but primarily led small groups for whole or half lessons in literacy. She produced her own materials and was very well regarded by the school. The school's leadership was interested in developing its SEN provision and in becoming a resourced school.

Planning was intended to be undertaken with the class teacher but, in reality, was left to the TA for completion in his or her own time. Much of the work with the statemented pupil took place outside the classroom, and although the pupil had been in school for a number of years, there was little evidence of interaction between him and his peers. During one visit, the pupil was observed in a mainstream history lesson. Most of the pupils in the class were academically able and the teacher's delivery and materials did not meet his needs. The TA sought to differentiate orally and then devised an alternative recording task. The class teacher was unable to comment about the progress of the statemented pupil, indicating that the TA 'knows all about him'. The TA felt that she held responsibility for the pupil but needed more support to make the curriculum accessible. Such support was timetabled through an advisory support teacher on a fortnightly basis, but due to ill health, this had not occurred for a substantial period of time. The class teacher and school management were very critical of this.

The second TA was observed teaching a small group of lower KS2 pupils on phonics-related work for half an hour in an open area. The pupils were on stages 2/3. She had prepared some attractive materials and had an excellent working relationship with the pupils. Much learning took place. Work was carefully planned, but it became apparent that if pupils faced unanticipated difficulties the TA lacked the skills to provide alternatives. She had received little training at this stage. She was very keen to develop her skills and noted, in conversation, that no-one talked with her in detail about her work.

The school's SENCO had an accurate awareness of the needs of pupils in the school and how staff interacted with them, and of the overdependence of statemented pupils on the TA for the statemented pupils, but had been advised not to tackle this issue. She, herself, was a full–time class teacher with other major responsibilities. Financial planning and timetabling were not within her direct sphere of influence.

In the high school there were a number of teaching assistants. They had originally worked for the LEA but had moved to the school's budget and management. After discussion about effective deployment of support staff, the school decided to move from support allocation to individual pupils, to support to departments, then to individuals where this was essential. (This was especially important for a pupil with ASD and for a pupil with marked physical and learning difficulties.) To enable this to happen the school increased spending on TAs.

Line management was through the SENCO and regular meetings were held with her. TAs were also paid to attend departmental meetings and whole-school INSET. Regular professional review took place and one TA was appointed as senior, working substantially on pupil recording systems using ICT. There had been initial concern about moving towards the new system and about ensuring that individual needs were met as indicated on a Statement. These were overcome and the TAs welcomed working in a department where they could enhance their skills.

Commentary

The situations described raise fundamental issues about ownership of support and the importance of all staff in contributing to the school's vision. In the primary school, the head teacher was full of commitment to meeting pupil needs but lacked knowledge about inclusion. For him, this was about having pupils on site, whereas the SENCO was seeking meaningful involvement within classes.

The greater size of the secondary school operation gave more scope for innovation but the issues in these scenarios are not about phase differences but rather about taking responsibility. The secondary school had made improvements and had developed a system that built ownership throughout the school, and actively supported TAs to play a valuable role. Interestingly, another school with a similar structure was recently inspected and, according to the Head of Learning Support, was initially viewed sceptically by the inspectors. It emerged with an excellent report as the advantages of departmentally based support within an overall co-ordinated framework became clear. One of the advantages of this way of working is that the inclusion of pupils with various needs is integrated into an holistic approach, with learning mentors and other staff supporting social inclusion working closely together.

Scenario 4 – leadership and responsibility

In two primary schools, resourced provision has long been established for up to 12 pupils with two specialist teachers and additional support staff. Staffing has been stable over a number of years.

In the first school, one of the two specialist teachers has acted as school SENCO but also has other senior management roles. Pupils have been increasingly included in mainstream classes, often with teaching assistant support, which is part of the resourced provision. Mainstream staff were unwelcoming at first but now accept the pupils as part of their responsibility and plan lessons accordingly; they recognise that support will not always be available and that it will not always be necessary. Teaching assistants throughout the school accept that they will be deployed flexibly and will offer support in the most appropriate manner. The dual role of specialist teacher/SENCO has been of great value in targeting support coherently and effectively.

In the second school, resourced provision was much more isolated. Although the teacher within the provision was a member of the senior management team her prime responsibility was 'additional provision'. Relatively little inclusion took place without additional support. A new head teacher was appointed who discussed the situation with the staff and LEA adviser. She recognised the skills and strengths of the additional staff but identified development areas:

- pupils from resourced provision interacted very little with mainstream peers;
- there was little professional interaction between mainstream and resourced provision staff;
- teaching groups within resourced provision were often either very small or small with an appreciable range of pupils in terms of chronological age and needs;
- there was a resistance to change on all sides and the provision was not widely regarded as part of whole-school philosophy and/or responsibility; and
- a small number of pupils in the mainstream would benefit from carefully structured language teaching as exemplified by resourced teachers.

Changes were introduced so that timetabling and resource allocation were looked at globally through the leadership team. Pupils with SEN were included more in mainstream, with or without support according to need. All pupils within resourced provision accessed the full National Curriculum. Teachers from within resourced provision occasionally taught mainstream classes and regularly taught small, mixed groups of mainstream and resourced pupils for Literacy and Numeracy Strategies.

Among the immediate improvements has been the increase in social integration of pupils from the resourced provision. Mainstream staff accept the role of the specialist teachers and believe that their expertise is more widely and effectively used. Pupils from the mainstream with significant language needs have benefited considerably. However, two issues remain: the first involves the complexity of the timetabling and the reduction in flexibility to make special provision according to emerging and sudden need; the second is that specialist staff, although generally supportive of changes, feel that there is reduced time to work with pupils with particular needs, especially those related to language and communication.

Commentary

The key aspects to emerge from these case studies relate to philosophy, ownership and inclusion. Whoever holds the ultimate responsibility for what occurs in additional provision (and there are different patterns nationally as to whether resourced provision has been fully delegated to the head teacher or is maintained centrally), there must be clear agreement and enactment of philosophy. Without senior leadership's full and active involvement, this is not likely to influence all practitioners, as it must. Mainstream staff should understand the rationale for small-group work but, equally, additional staff need to recognise their limitations and the wider context of inclusion. Time for joint consideration and reflection of combined practice is essential. There must be a balance between the needs of the individual for specific input and inclusion. There should be a balance between system and structure and the ability to respond to needs that change quickly.

Scenario 5 – best value

Schools' ability to identify and rationalise their spending and subsequent approach to meeting SEN is described in three studies of average-size primary schools. In all cases, the percentage of pupils identified as having SEN was between 20 per cent and 32 per cent and the number of pupils with Statements was slightly higher than the national average.

In the first case, the head teacher was actively involved in SEN finance and overview. The bulk of spending paid for a designated SENCO who carried out individual withdrawal work for three days of the week and spent a fourth day on assessment, as there was high mobility in the area. The other substantial spending was on the time the head teacher spent on SEN-related issues through case conferences, support for parents and administration.

The SENCO worked with pupils at stage three on an intensive daily approach based on Reading Recovery. Initial progress by many – but not all – pupils was good, but there was little recorded evidence of whether/how this was maintained in mainstream classes. Mainstream staff were resentful of the role of the SENCO and felt that the investment of her time with pupils at stage three meant that they received no support with pupils at earlier stages. The intensive nature of the SENCOs input with a small number of pupils each half-term meant that only a small number of pupils with SEN received support. There was initial reluctance to arrange for TAs to provide for small groups for literacy using national materials as this was perceived by some to undermine the role of specialist teaching.

Although there was clear accountability for spending no attempt was made to ascertain whether this was the most effective use of staffing and, therefore, value for money.

In the second school, the head teacher had to appoint a new SENCO, and deliberately appointed a young, up-and-coming, good teacher, particularly in relation to pupil management, differentiation and interpersonal skills. He then arranged for her to have training to develop specialist skills. In terms of budget, he provided a small amount of release time that was spent working with pupils and/or observing in class to ensure familiarity with all pupils on the SEN register and their classrooms. The rest of the delegated finance was spent on employing TAs who worked with pupils at stage two and an external teacher to provide additional input for pupils at stage three. This worked very effectively except that liaison and administration were difficult for the SENCO and required the head teacher to cover her for a lesson each week.

In the third school, the head teacher was the SENCO. She worked directly with pupils for three sessions a week and led reviews. Additional support was also provided by 'topping up' the hours of the reception nursery nurse. Individual Education Plans (IEPs) were of good quality and were monitored by the head as a regular part of whole-school planning and monitoring. Withdrawal sessions were long, at an hour and a quarter, but were justified in terms of organisation of mainstream classes and in not returning pupils half way through a lesson. The nursery nurse was unaware that her additional hours were from the SEN budget as the head felt that by working with all pupils she would, *per se*, be helping those with SEN.

Commentary

In all three cases, the head teachers of the schools had considered the budgets and could account for SEN spending. However, evaluation systems were as yet underdeveloped. In some instances, the provision of additional support failed to contribute to whole-school development and may have promoted seclusion rather than inclusion.

It is a major step forward to know how budgets are spent but in the context of inclusion the best and the worst practice can look the same on paper. Where money is deployed across all aspects of a school, and additional support deployed flexibly, all staff may be undertaking their role effectively and best practice may exist. Equally, the finances may be dispersed with no impact. Reporting spending patterns to the Governing Body is important but reports also need to address pupil progress, impact, alternative intervention, best value and value for money.

What are the ways forward?

Issues concerning the school's ability to support its most vulnerable pupils will remain contentious if there is a lack of clarity about who has responsibility for meeting their needs. In order to take forward the significant amount of good practice that already exists, there needs to be:

- wider agreement about what we mean by inclusion and the features which make a school inclusive (as noted in the Audit Commission Report (2002);
- clear leadership and commitment to meeting the needs of all pupils which involves systems for meeting SENs being part of other school systems and not separate from them;
- flexibility in working, with a greater emphasis on team working, shared responsibility and shared planning between mainstream and specialist staff;
- sharing of good practice;
- careful consideration of the use of additional resources delegated to the school;
- evaluation of schools which celebrates inclusivity and academic standards and is based on a wider use of value added (as suggested by the Scottish HMI Report *Count Us In* (HMI 2002);
- further opportunities for staff development and movement between mainstream and specialist sectors;
- more rigorous self-evaluation with greater clarity about the role played by all parties, led by the school's leadership team which includes the SENCO or INCO (Inclusion Co-ordinator) but is not led by them, and integrated into other mechanisms for evaluation wherever possible; and
- a move away from Statements of SEN towards more flexible funding.

4

Social inclusion: supporting schools to help themselves

Gill Henderson

Editors' introduction

Gill Henderson considers how support services can move from being 'crisis led', taking on the problems that schools encounter, to being proactive in ensuring that teachers feel confident and competent in responding to a wider range of difference. Where schools have to deal with complex difficulties requiring support from a variety of agencies, she stresses the importance of interagency working based on a shared infrastructure rather than fragmented multiagency inputs. A number of small-scale projects are described that illustrate this way of working and take advantage of short-term funding streams. Henderson notes that the sustainability of the resulting capacity for inclusion arising from these projects is at risk because of the uncertainty of continued funding.

Introduction

Inclusive education is a fundamental principle that underpins all recent educational legislation and is clearly reinforced by the SEN Code of Practice (*SEN and Disability Act 2001*) and the Disability Rights Commission Code of Practice for Schools (*Disability Discrimination Act 1994, Part 4*). While most schools now feel relatively well equipped to cater for the majority of pupils with an increasing range of learning difficulties, those pupils who continue to present the greatest challenges to teachers are those who display emotional, behavioural and social difficulties. There are various services, both within and outside the LEA, with whom the school can engage in order to enlist support; however, the potential value of the use of these services is often diminished on two counts.

Firstly, the interventions are often crisis-led, which results in the guidance being necessarily reactive. In order to develop a proactive culture, with a focus on early intervention strategies, schools must be supported to develop an ethos and framework in which teachers can meet the needs of these pupils with both confidence and competence. This will then prevent the creation of a culture of dependency in which the external agency 'treats' the problem for the school. To a certain extent, it could be argued that this approach was encouraged by the first SEN Code of Practice (DfEE 1994) in which involvement of external agencies was at stage three, after all actions by the school had failed to address the problem. However, this situation is redressed in the current Code where a gradual response that encompasses an array of strategies is recommended, so that 'speedy access to LEA support services for one-off or occasional advice ... may make it possible to provide effective intervention without the need for regular or ongoing input from external agencies' (DfES 2001a; 5: 49; 6: 57).

Secondly, the reason for the behavioural problems may be complex and a number of different agencies may be involved, hence the terminology 'multiagency working'. This can, however, mean different agencies supporting the child, the family and the school without clear communication channels, and a subsequent reduction in both effectiveness and efficiency. In this climate, short-term solutions may be provided, but continued difficulties are often inevitable in the longer term. It could be argued, therefore, that *interagency* working, where all involved services are committed to working collaboratively within a firmly established infrastructure, will promote a far more successful way of ensuring that appropriate support can be both provided and sustained.

This chapter describes different projects that demonstrate how different agencies, both within and outside the LEA, have worked with schools to help them become self-sufficient in meeting the needs of pupils with emotional, behavioural and social needs, and how collaborative working can be proactive in promoting positive behaviour.

Case study 1

Pupil mentoring: early intervention in an infant school (key support services: family support workers (linked to the educational welfare service), educational psychology service)

This initiative was developed in a large infant school serving an area of social deprivation in a large town. Many of the children attending the school come from families where there are restricted opportunities to play and to learn to interact appropriately with peers. Language development is often limited and the children are unable to articulate their feelings adequately. A particularly difficult cohort of reception pupils coincided with a change in the way in which the LEA delegated funding for SEN. This gave the head teacher and governing body the opportunity to explore more creative ways of using the funding for SEN pupils. The school decided to take two key steps: first, to appoint a full-time teaching assistant as a pupil mentor who had a clear remit to support the pupils whose emotional, behavioural and social needs were causing most concern; and second, to review how the curriculum was being delivered. From the start of the project, the decision was made that support would be focused on the pupils and not on classroom support. The school's educational psychologist was enlisted to evaluate the impact of the project as it evolved.

The pupil mentor

Individual pupils who are exhibiting emotional, social and/or behavioural difficulties are withdrawn for 'special' time with the pupil mentor; however, they are not withdrawn at the same time each week. This ensures that curriculum entitlement is not affected and allows flexibility for crisis interventions – it also prevents pupils from expecting to be withdrawn. The head teacher and pupil mentor meet formally each week in order to discuss which pupils will access the support and to draw up the timetable; this is closely linked to the work of the Family Support Worker who may also be involved with the families. The 'special' work with the pupil mentor takes place in the library. It involves practical activities and games that target the pupils' strengths and interests and the resources used are special to that child. As the pupils take part in the activities they are encouraged to talk about themselves; in many cases the pupils do not have the language or the confidence to articulate what is causing their behaviour. One of the fundamental principles of the project is to provide a means of developing the pupils' confidence in order to identify the cause of the problem, and so begin to address their difficulties.

The pupils view these sessions neither as a treat nor a punishment; more crucially, they present an opportunity to break a cycle of negativity, working with a trusted adult who will support them. All interventions are recorded in a diary and, in some instances, this has provided essential information that has resulted in further support for the family from the Social Services Department. As a result, there has been a marked decrease in inappropriate behaviours and further escalation has been prevented. Many parents have noted a similar pattern of improved behaviour at home. The need for further specialist support has been reduced, as have the high levels of stress experienced by teachers, pupils and parents when behaviour becomes difficult to manage.

Curriculum review

Concurrent with the introduction of the pupil mentor, the school undertook an evaluation of the way in which the curriculum was delivered. Different approaches to teaching and learning were analysed with an emphasis on visual, aural and kinaesthetic activities. The principles of 'Hi-scope' in the nursery were extended to the reception class and Year 1, speaking and listening were planned into all aspects of the school day and art activities were incorporated into the Literacy and Numeracy strategy. Expectations remained high, but modes of delivery were altered to ensure that the pupils remained motivated and involved in their learning. This, too, had a positive impact, not only on behaviour across the whole school but also on academic achievements as evidenced through improved SATs (Standardised Attainment Tests) results.

Summary

A school-based initiative, focusing on early intervention that has successfully enabled teachers and support staff to more effectively meet the needs of children who, from an early age, present with a variety of challenging behaviours. Consequently, this has resulted in much more focused and collaborative inter-agency support for those children who continue to have the most significant and complex needs. Although data to support the impact of this project is difficult to quantify, SATs results have increased – and two pupils with Statements for EBD far exceeded their teacher's original expectations. The number of exclusions has reduced – as has the need to use higher-level sanctions. The school is generally much calmer and the pupil mentor is now more able to work with groups of pupils to develop social skills, rather than supporting individual pupils at times of crisis.

Case study 2

Developing behaviour policy and practice in a primary school: sharing good practice (key support services: Educational Psychology Service, Behaviour Support Service, Learning Support Advisory Team, Educational Welfare Service; monitoring by the Education Advisory Service)

This project was established in a rural primary school that served a particularly diverse and challenging catchment area. The focus of the project was to assist the school to generate a positive learning environment where pupils with emotional, behavioural and social needs could develop self-management skills and staff could use a collaborative approach to problem-solving. The longer-term aims were to provide the school with an infrastructure, which would promote self-sufficiency in meeting the needs of pupils presenting with a range of challenging behaviours, and also to produce materials that could be used to disseminate this approach to other schools.

The Educational Psychology Service was pivotal to the project, although its success was also due to the links maintained with other involved services, particularly the Learning Support Advisory Teacher, the Behaviour Support Teacher and the Educational Welfare Officer.

The project commenced with a behavioural audit to support a whole-school review of behaviour policy and practice, based on the premise that the aim was to be responsive to the needs of the school, rather than imposing predetermined models. As a result, a new policy that involved all staff was designed and key points for action were identified, based on the general principle that a school community that can solve problems together is a learning and developing organisation. Within this framework, the school agreed on a range of initiatives to promote good behaviour and reduce disaffection:

- developing emotional literacy through circle time;
- supporting lunchtime supervisors;
- providing staff support teams;
- peer mediation;
- anger management; and
- supporting parents to promote positive behaviour at home.

This was further supported by a review of the effectiveness of Individual Education Plans (IEPs) and a move to reinforce and extend existing work with parents. These activities were actively supported and reinforced by the Learning Support Advisory Teacher, the Behaviour Support Teacher and the Educational Welfare Officer working with staff and pupils. The planning and implementation of the project took place over the autumn and spring terms; the summer term focused on review, evaluation and the preparation of materials for publication.

An evaluation of the project indicated that pupils had ownership of the school rules and had begun to reflect of the impact on others when they were not followed. Staff felt empowered to deal with difficult situations, pupils felt more secure (with a subsequent increase in self-esteem), lunchtimes were calmer and supervisors more confident.

Support materials were then published, available either as 'stand alone' materials or as part of a training package. This has enabled a number of schools to successfully develop similar initiatives within the context of their own learning environment.

Summary

This project, which was based on an initially high level of intervention and support, had the longer-term aim of promoting self-sufficiency. The key factor to success was ensuring that a secure infrastructure was firmly embedded in the work of the school, so that the good practice could be sustained and further developed. Standards of attainment rose considerably, as evidenced by the end-of-key-stage testing, and behaviour throughout the school improved. Analysis of the KS2 SATs results showed continuing and significant improvement, with all targets set being exceeded.

Case study 3

A family-based approach to promoting positive behaviour in a cluster of primary schools (key support services: Educational Welfare Service, Social Services)

A collaborative interagency approach to promoting positive behaviour through family-based support formed the basis of this project. It was a time-limited initiative, originally set up to support a cluster of schools in a rural market town characterised by social deprivation. At the end of the agreed timescale (one year), the project was moved to set up a similar support network in an urban setting, focusing on a number of primary schools serving another area of social deprivation. Early indications in both the rural and the urban setting were that one of the objectives – to promote self-sufficiency within the schools to sustain the outcomes – would not be achievable. This was due to the crucial role of the key worker in providing ongoing support to the families and linking with the other agencies that supported them outside of the school environment. However, both projects have since identified different ways of sustaining the initiative through alternative funding streams in order to ensure that the invaluable work can continue.

The development of the project hinged on the appointment of an educational welfare officer who was based at a local community centre. The schools involved in the project identified pupils who had emotional, behavioural and/or social needs that were impacting on their learning. The educational welfare officer began by establishing a network with all local agencies from the police and social services to health visitors, housing and furniture schemes and youth workers. Links with the families of the children identified by the schools were established and this led to some work in the local secondary school attended by siblings. The close involvement of the 'patch' educational welfare officer provided essential links and also proved to be invaluable in terms of local knowledge.

The project continues to be supported through funding from the Single Regeneration Budget (SRB) in both settings and, in the urban area, the team was extended to include two additional posts. As would be anticipated, there were major differences between the needs of the families in the urban and rural areas that impacted on the project work. The influence of drugs and illegal substances was much more prevalent in the urban area, whereas alcohol had been a prime factor in many of the difficulties encountered by families in the rural project. A greater history of disaffection in the urban area, reinforced by the negative educational experiences of parents, necessitated a major shift to identify the children earlier. A key factor appeared to be transition – either from preschool playgroup or nursery into the reception class; from the infant school into the junior school; and from junior to secondary phase. The project, therefore, focused on preschool and early nurturing, infant transition to junior, and transfer from Year 6 into Year 7. Strong links were forged with the local mothers/toddlers groups and with the preschool playgroups in order to gain the trust and respect of the future prospective parents of school children. Participation in 'Circle Time' at the infant school ensured that every child would know the project worker before transition to the junior school. Circle-time activities continued in the junior school with the Year 3 pupils, running alongside existing work instigated by the two schools. A mentoring programme was introduced at the local secondary school, which involved training Year 9 pupils to act as peer mentors for the new Year 7 pupils. The success of this scheme (as evidenced by the decrease in exclusions) was due to the careful selection of mentors who were chosen on the basis of where they lived, street credibility and shyness – not because of their likelihood of becoming a prefect at a later date. Work with the social services department through the Children's Fund enabled crime prevention and environmental issues such as graffiti and vandalism to be tackled. Work is now underway to make a bid to the local Sure Start project to secure funding for three additional workers to develop support for the transition into primary schooling, while collaboration with the Youth Offending Service will target specific interventions with pupils who come from families with a history of criminality.

The project has not only made a huge impact on the pupils, but also on the local community. Pupils have demonstrated significant development, both in terms of their academic achievements, as well as improved social and emotional wellbeing. The project worker is now accepted within the community and is viewed as an independent body, not employed by the school; thus, when a pupil has a problem at school, the worker can investigate without prejudice and report back to the family who are much more willing to work co-operatively. All of the project workers have gained trust and respect from the families they work with, and those who refuse intervention are the exception rather than the rule. Two major local supermarkets have also played strategic roles in the success of the project by offering training facilities during the evening and providing a room for a 'Drop In' session for parents on a Friday morning. This has provided a non-threatening, neutral environment and is ideal for the disaffected parents who would not actively seek support.

Summary

An extremely successful project that has made a significant impact on both the community and the children and young people within that community. The importance of gaining the trust and respect of the project workers has been the motivating force that ensures effective interagency collaboration. One of the major drawbacks for this project (and for many other similar initiatives throughout the country) is the insecurity about future development, as reliance on relatively short-term funding streams continues.

Case study 4

Successful re-integration of KS3 pupils at risk of exclusion (key support services: Education Advisory Service, Education Welfare Service)

This initiative was initially set up as a pilot project by the LEA in order to provide early, intensive provision to promote good behaviour for disaffected pupils in KS3 at risk of exclusion. Consequently, the LEA provides the funding in the main, although participating schools contribute £1,000 per pupil. The maximum number of pupils per cohort is six and there are two cohorts per term. Staffing comprises two full-time behaviour support teachers and one full-time support assistant. The project is accommodated in a local youth centre and facilities include a large activity area and kitchen, a classroom (which ideally should be larger for the purpose), indoor sports hall, soundproof music-room and a shared office. There is also storage space, ample car parking and an outside activity area and playing field.

The intervention is based on the notion of a study course. The components of the course consist of preliminary work, four-week attendance by the pupils at the centre, followed by in-school support for the pupils by the centre staff. Participating schools are requested to release teachers or teaching assistants to spend time with the pupils at the centre, not only as part of their professional development, but also in order that schools retain ownership of the pupil and demonstrate commitment to helping them succeed; this is also an important factor in successful re-integration.

Preliminary work

This begins with the identification and referral of pupils by the schools, in conjunction with the LEA Inclusion and Behaviour Support Manager. When placement has been agreed, the centre staff take the lead and begin to collate all appropriate additional information. Pupils are observed in their school environment and there is a meeting with an identified key worker from the school. A home visit also takes place to meet the parents/carers and the pupil in order to discuss the programme of support.

The four-week course

Pupils attend the centre for five hours each day. The curriculum includes the core subjects and elements of most foundation subjects. Some sessions are taught by members of the Education Advisory Service in order to provide expertise in more specialist subjects, such as music, ICT and PSHE; there is also a programme of outdoor education. Breaks and lunchtimes are carefully structured in order to focus on the development of social skills. The personal development programme includes anger management, dealing with conflict, de-escalating situations, speaking to others appropriately and working collaboratively. There is an emphasis on building group rapport and trust, following school rules and coping with pressure. A continuous programme of reinforcement of behaviour management strategies underpins the course as a whole, supported by timetabled circle time.

Attendance, progress and achievements are meticulously recorded –

celebration of academic success is another key aspect of building self-esteem and self-confidence. There are planned visits by a range of professionals and the voluntary sector involving talks, support work and mentoring for the pupils, both during the course and upon return to school. Parents/carers are also encouraged to attend the centre on a regular basis and another important element of the course are the visits by the key workers from the schools involved.

Re-integration

Prior to the pupils returning to school, the centre staff provide a written report for the school and the parents/carers. This summarises the course content and describes the attendance and progress made by the pupil, it also suggests strategies for supporting the pupil upon return to school. A meeting takes place with the pupil, their parent/carer and the key worker from the school to discuss strategies and support for the re-integration; further meetings with the school also take place in order to agree negotiated support.

Upon return to school, the centre staff support all pupils, taking account of their individual needs and the needs of the school. The support includes involvement in setting up individual pupil programmes and targets, one-to-one sessions, withdrawal from 'hot spots' and also for relevant activities at the centre. Teachers are also supported and advice is provided on linking rewards to the whole-school behaviour and discipline policy, ensuring that they are appropriate to the individual. Channels of communication are set up between home and school and it is ensured that pupils who have been previous non-attenders arrive at school. The progress of each pupil is regularly monitored and meetings are set up to review progress formally.

Support for the parents/carers is an important element, both during the course and after return to school. This includes regular updates on the pupil's progress via telephone calls, visits and postcards. Offers are made to accompany parents/carers to meetings at school or with other agencies such as Social Services or the Child and Family Service. Advice on encouraging attendance at school and in managing behaviour at home is provided and, where appropriate, advice in developing and consistently implementing organisational skills is also made available.

Summary

This continues to be an extremely successful project that has had a significant impact on the amount of time pupils remain in their schools. The Education Advisory Service has been instrumental in ensuring a range of curricular activities for the pupils, but the crucial success factor has been the intensive work to meet the emotional, social and behavioural needs of the pupils by the centre staff and the focused approach to interagency collaboration. At the time of writing, 48 pupils have attended the centre, 38 boys and 10 girls. The ability range has been very wide and has included high-achieving pupils as well as those with significant learning difficulties. Of the 48 pupils, the majority have been successfully re-integrated into local mainstream schools and only three have subsequently been excluded.

Conclusion

Initiatives similar to those described in the case studies above are being replicated in many schools and LEAs throughout the country and, while the contexts of these case studies may not be relevant to all schools (for example, issues relating to rural deprivation), this does not detract from the fundamental principles of promoting positive behaviour and reducing disaffection that are applicable to all schools and LEAs.

Access to short-term funding, such as the Standards Fund and the Pupil Retention Grant, formed the basis on which some of the projects described above, and many comparable projects across the country, have been developed. These are funding streams that are no longer ring-fenced and which, in many instances, are likely to be swallowed up in the face of other priorities. It is crucial, therefore, to ensure that any projects have self-sufficiency built in as an identified objective in order to ensure the longer-term benefits.

At the beginning of this chapter, the need to respond reactively, rather than proactively, is identified as one of the aspects that appears to diminish the effectiveness of support services in meeting the needs of pupils with emotional, social and behavioural difficulties. The case studies described in this chapter illustrate how, in different ways, all staff have increased their knowledge and understanding about the needs of the pupils; this has, in turn, facilitated earlier recognition and more effective intervention. Consequently, this has enabled the support services working in the schools to work together far more efficiently in targeting need. Equally, those initiatives with an interagency focus have clearly demonstrated how a collaborative approach can make a significant impact on not only the behaviour and achievements of the pupils involved but also on their families and the local community.

The aim and scope of the current DfES SEN Action Programme (1998) recognises many of the attendant issues described here, particularly in relation to early identification and multiagency (or interagency) working. Real progress will depend crucially not only on the commitment of all involved agencies, but also on the establishment of a firm infrastructure, supported by secure budgetary arrangements, that facilitates strategic collaborative planning. Without this, the ad hoc approach will continue; short-term projects will raise expectations and the opportunities for longer-term benefits will not be realised.

5

Interagency working: supporting school refusers

Christine Salter

Editors' introduction

Christine Salter describes the work undertaken in Bexley to address the needs of a group of school refusers, often referred to as the 'disappeared'. These are pupils who regularly fall between two services, and in her chapter she demonstrates how this can be avoided by developing trans-agency work across education and mental health. The title of the service, Total Support for Learning Service, is particularly revealing, reflecting the principle of one agency working inside, rather than alongside, another. The work she describes is project-based, preventative and community-based, demonstrating many of the features of a well-developed service. She uses individual pupil case studies to demonstrate effectiveness. Evaluation is a strong component of this work and, as a result, we learn many important lessons about effective planning.

The background

Bexley Council is a London Borough with a school population of 40,000, a high level of home ownership and areas of socioeconomic and social deprivation. On a range of indicators, such as percentage of pupils with statements of SEN, Bexley is average.

Since the introduction of the first SEN Code of Practice in 1994, Bexley has considered requests for statutory assessment through a multidisciplinary panel. In parallel, a Children Out of School Panel has endeavoured to plan for pupils not attending school or at risk of absence, for whatever reason. Analysis of data from 1994 to 1997 showed that a small but significant number of pupils who refused to attend school were passed between panels. This group of pupils often functioned well academically; their problem was poor attendance. The pupils were not excluded, did not present as disruptive and absence was often authorised on medical grounds. Statutory assessment was conducted for some pupils but did not provide the immediacy of response required, and it proved difficult to implement a Statement for a pupil who stayed at home.

In 1996/97 representatives of the local Child and Adolescent Mental Health Service (CAMHS) met with education department staff about the steady stream of referrals from GPs of pupils with 'school phobia'. Problems were often well-established before the referral was made, and there was little CAMHS could do to treat 'school phobia' in the absence of a school service to implement recommendations. An opportunity arose through the Standards Fund to establish a project focused on the learning needs of pupils with mental health problems. The Service was established alongside the Secondary Behaviour Support Service in September 1999; it is transferring to the Educational Psychology Service at the time of writing.

Defining school refusal

Berg (1997) defines school refusal as

> a condition characterised by reluctance and often outright refusal to go to school in a child who: (1) seeks the comfort and security of home, preferring to stay close to parental figures, especially during school hours; (2) displays evidence of emotional upset when faced with the prospect of having to attend school, although this may only take the form of unexplained physical symptoms; (3) manifests no severe antisocial tendencies, apart from possible aggressiveness when attempts are made to force school attendance; and (4) does not attempt to conceal the problem from parents.

Boys and girls are equally affected and there is no relationship to social class. Children with the condition may have anxiety, depression and other disorders. School refusal often affects 11–13-year-olds but may be present from 5–15 years.

The four categories defined by Kearney and Silverman (1990) are helpful to teachers and support workers as they focus on what the child or young person gains from school refusal:

1. avoidance of specific fearfulness or general over-anxiousness related to the school setting. This includes cases where one or more particular features of a school (toilets, corridors, test-taking situations, specific teachers) are feared;
2. escape from aversive social situations. This concerns problems based upon negative relationships with others (teachers and/or peers), particularly

where an element of evaluation is perceived to be present;

3. attention-getting or separation anxiety behaviour. This may be reflected by somatic complaints or tantrums where the child seeks to remain at home with the parent or important other;

4. rewarding experiences provided out of school. Non-attendance is rewarding in that it offers opportunities for the child to engage in preferred activities such as watching television or associating with friends. This category includes those usually considered to be truants.

Incidence

In view of the broad and complex nature of school refusal, it is not surprising that there is no clear information in the literature on incidence. Meltzer and Gatward (2000) found that children with an emotional, conduct or other mental disorder were twice as likely to be away from school for 11 days or more as other children (19% compared with 8%) with emotional disorders alone accounting for 25 per cent of pupils away for 11 days or more.

Between 4 and 5 per cent of children and adolescents have been found to suffer from separation anxiety to the extent of their anxiety being termed a disorder, and 75 per cent of children so affected were also school refusers (Masi *et al.* 2001).

Intervention

In a study in which 56 children were either treated with cognitive-behavioural therapy or social attention, Last *et al.* (1998) concluded that traditional educational and supportive treatment methods were as effective in returning children to school as highly structured cognitive-behavioural therapy. However, this may not be the case when the pupil has a specific disorder such as separation anxiety (Masi *et al. op. cit.*). This illustrates the need for CAMHS involvement when purposeful work within education is not effective in re-establishing a pupil in school.

Behaviour programmes for school refusers are primarily exposure-based, desensitising pupils in a variety of ways (King and Ollendick 1997). Evidence for enforced return appears strong, at least in the case of the children for whom it has been selected. For example, Kearney and Beasley (1994) employed enforced return in 11.6 per cent of cases, but these cases were 100 per cent successful. Similarly, Blagg and Yule (1984) achieved 93.3 per cent success with forced return in comparison with home tuition (10%) and hospitalised (37.5%) groups.

The children in these studies were not randomly allocated. Elliott (1999) advises caution in using enforced return, particularly in the case of highly anxious pupils. Certainly schools may find a more graduated approach less distressing and more acceptable ethically. Cognitive-behavioural therapy is an approach that encourages the child to identify thoughts and beliefs that lead to anxious feelings and to learn to view events from a perspective that decreases their anxiety. Last *et al.* (1998) divided 56 school-refusing children into two groups: one received cognitive-behaviour therapy; the other received educational support. Both groups improved after 12 weeks, with no differences between them. In the absence of further research, the aspects of cognitive-behaviour therapy that might help specific children are not known.

Children are most likely to go back to school when they realise that their parents are determined to effect a return. Parents tend to see school problems as causative, but a change of school seldom makes a difference (Elliott 1999). Kearney and Silverman (1995) describe five typical family situations where children are refusing school:

- coercive, and marked by conflict;
- enmeshed and overdependent;
- detached, with little interaction among family members;
- isolated, with little interaction outside of family grouping; and
- a healthy family with a child with an individualised psychopathology.

Elliott reports that the effectiveness of family therapy in returning school refusers to school continues to be unclear and that 'pharmacological treatments for school refusal continue to be under-researched and controversial' (p. 1007). Elliott advocates a commonsense approach:

> where refusal is considered to be primarily the result of a strongly phobic reaction to being in school, systematic desensitisation and immediate or gradual exposure to school are recommended. Where it is largely a means of avoiding school and social and/or evaluative situations, modelling, role-play, and cognitive therapy are suggested. In cases where the problem results from a desire to obtain caregiver attention, parent training and contingency management are deemed appropriate. Finally, where refusal is considered to be largely the result of the attractiveness of domestic pleasures, family therapy and contingency contracting are advocated. Where there are multiple functional conditions involving a combination of the four categories, a number of procedures may need to be used in combination.

The approaches taken in the Bexley project were based on knowledge of existing literature and substantial experience of working with school refusers.

The role of the school and alternative provision

Vigilance and sensitivity on the part of staff working in the school and effective management of situations as they arise may prevent school refusal from developing. For example, school refusal is often triggered by a period of absence for reasons of physical ill-health. The attitude and approach of school staff confronted with school refusal and enabling a pupil to return to school is key, as is drawing up and implementing contingency plans in case of panic attacks.

Outcomes in adulthood

In some cases there is a genetic and familial predisposition that presents as school phobia in childhood. Looking back from adulthood, a number of adults with agoraphobia were school refusers (Perugi *et al*. 1988). Looking forward into adulthood, at least 33 per cent of clinical cases continue to experience severe emotional and social difficulties in adulthood (Berg and Jackson 1985).

While the studies described the most severe cases, they are reminders that for some children school refusal may be an indicator of potential lifelong mental health problems. It would be beyond the expertise of most staff working in schools and education support services to assess and determine intervention programmes for this group. Partnership working with CAMHS is essential.

The Total Support for Learning Service (TSL)

The aim of the service is to enable pupils who do not attend school for psychological reasons to do so. The budget for the service in 2002/03 was £112,000, excluding management, educational psychology, education welfare and other agency time.

The service began with one experienced teacher with a background in secondary education, one project worker and two support assistants, and time from the teacher in charge of the Secondary Behaviour Support Service. An experienced EP with a clinical background initially provided several sessions a week for two terms to provide consultation to the service, to work within CAMHS to enhance liaison between agencies and to develop partnership between the TSL and CAMHS. This proved an important catalyst despite some tensions that are discussed later in this chapter. A CAMHS clinician also provided monthly consultation services.

As the service was grant-funded, and funding could only be agreed towards the end of each financial year, staff security of employment was an issue. Information about the service was circulated in leaflet form and included in literature about services. The groups most likely to refer pupils (CAMHS, Education Welfare, Educational Psychology and the panels described above) had been involved in the establishment of the service and were well-positioned to make appropriate referrals. However, the most effective communications about the functioning of the service and the requirements of potential partners were those around individual pupils.

Referrals followed the formal protocols generally required in the Authority. Initial direct contact between the potential referrer and the head of service proved an essential addition, whether to redirect referral efforts or to establish early conjoint working. Criteria for referral were rigorously applied. The principles on which the service was built were: availability, flexibility and persistence. The service maintained a curriculum focus at all times. Partnership with school and college staff was fundamental to its work.

The work of the TSL Service

At the time of writing, the TSL has been providing services for three years. There have been 115 referrals to the service and 104 pupils taken on. Analysis of the first 60 closed cases shows that the service worked with pupils for an average of eight months (range one to 24 months). The programme for each pupil was determined at an initial planning meeting, but an unintended effect of taking on too many referrals was that programmes were curtailed by workloads. Progress was reviewed systematically, resulting in the withdrawal of services where support was 'not well used'. This was a hard and unpopular decision to make. The types of support received by pupils are set out at the end of this chapter.

This chapter is focused on the work of a specialised support service, but the part played by the school was fundamental to the success of programmes, and to the ability of the service to identify cases where the project could not assist. It was not possible to intervene positively in any case where the school did not engage fully in endeavouring to re-integrate the pupil. In extreme cases, the school had taken a non-attending pupil off roll. Services could not be provided until a school place had been found, and for a variety of reasons, this was not easily achieved.

Joe

Joe attended primary school well, and had no learning difficulties. After a few weeks in secondary school he felt unsafe, reporting that money was being demanded of him and that other boys were aggressive. He stopped attending. Joe's parents took him to their GP who referred him to CAMHS. While on the waiting list, Joe talked of suicide. The Education Welfare Service asked the TSL Project to become involved. TSL began to re-integrate Joe very gradually, aiming at some attendance each day. Joe was motivated to attend school. He helped set his weekly targets. The school made time and space for Joe and gave positive feedback whenever appropriate. With a TSL worker's support, his parents maintained a structured routine when Joe was at home and Joe learned to interact with them more positively.

The TSL support assistant took Joe to and from school, keeping this activity separate from support for his parents. The CAMHS primary mental health worker worked with the family and with Joe. Everyone was persistent.

Joe remains a nervous boy, but has re-established himself in school; he mixes with his peers in school and out of school. The relationship between him and his parents is positive.

Susan

My daughter's difficulties started in her first year at secondary school, when she was ill. She was bullied about her illness ... Susan became seriously depressed and hurt herself. She needed in-patient treatment at an adolescent psychiatric unit.

I was very surprised by the TSL approach. They spent several sessions talking to her and taking her on little outings. I now realise that this gradual introduction is one of the most successful aspects, as they were building trust, and getting to know her, and without that all their efforts would have been in vain ... School was not even discussed until they were confident with each other. The TSL staff were 100 per cent sympathetic and understanding, but used a steady, gentle, guiding hand to ease Susan back into education – never any pressure. Susan resumed her education at a college of further education, which had a flexible timetable and fewer expectations for academic success, allowing her to sit just a few GCSEs in the first year, part-time.

The end result is more than we could ever have hoped for. She is doing A levels this year. She is willingly involved with social activities. She still has her emotional problems and anxiety about new people, but this is slowly diminishing. The TSL workers gave Susan a purpose for getting up, and a glimpse of a future ahead, where previously it had been bleak.

Evaluation

Evaluation of the progress of each pupil towards achieving weekly targets was integral to the service. It was intended that evaluation be rigorous and include pre- and post-intervention data collection, and sufficient information about the activities undertaken to enable service managers to reflect and build upon 'what works'. Problems arose from the short time-frame afforded by one-year funding. The service forged ahead too soon, and those conceptualising the service did not have time to establish evaluation protocols. There was insufficient clinical time to carry out pre-testing and no school or education welfare time to research the detail behind attendance figures.

As the service adopted policies, procedures and patterns of working, methods of systematic data collection of basic information, activities undertaken and costs were established. Pre- and post-intervention attendance data were sought. Accurate data proved unexpectedly elusive. Preliminary evaluation of the project showed an apparent drop in school attendance for some of the pupils perceived as successful in improving their attendance. This anomaly arose from the variety of ways in which absence was recorded.

It emerged that some school refusers were excused school by GPs, in the absence of referral for treatment for their perceived stress or distress, and on the reports of parents alone. This issue has been taken up by the Community Paediatrician advising the service.

Evaluation of progress in terms of a pupil's mental health was the last element to be established, despite it having been the first priority. The systematic use of tests and protocols to provide measures of anxiety, attitudes to school attendance, social competence, depression and stress proved impracticable. Some measure of personal change being essential, the Health of the National Outcome Scales for Children and Adolescents (HoNOSCA) were adopted. (For HoNOSCA, and critiques of the approach, see Gowers *et al.* 1998).

Each pupil with whom the TSL Project worked was rated on the basis of referral information and background reports at entry. Ratings were retrospective from papers for the first 35 pupils. Exit ratings were made on the basis of third-party reports at closure, objective evidence and key worker opinion. The HoNOSCA criteria are loosely defined and intended for evaluation within one setting. It proved necessary for ratings to be conducted by the same two professionals for all cases: the Teacher in Charge of the TSL Project and the Principal Educational Psychologist. No claim is made that this system was rigorous – but it proved achievable, informative and made sense to staff. Finally, each pupil completing the intervention programme with the TSL, or leaving the service, was allocated a descriptive outcome category: school attendance, court action, education other than at school, or referral on (such as for special educational needs assessment).

Findings

The average age of pupils at the time of referral was 12.85 years (range 11 to 16 years). There were equal numbers of boys and girls. Ninety per cent of the pupils remained on the roll of their original school while working with the service. Statutory assessment had been requested in respect of six pupils, one of whom had a Statement. Twenty-four pupils (40%) reported being bullied in school at the time of their engagement with the service.

In-class support was provided to 43 pupils (72%), time ranging from one hour to 75 hours. Out-of-school activities were provided to 43 pupils, time ranging from 12.3 hours to 88 hours. Liaison was undertaken in all cases, time involvement ranging from one hour to 92 hours. In all but two cases, the service worked with parents, time ranging from one hour to 75 hours. Staff transported pupils to and from activities or school in 34 cases (57%).

Cost analysis was based on the time/salary costs of staff, travel and equipment/activity costs, and therefore a crude measure. The average cost per pupil of intervention was £1072 with a range from £17 to £3880. Statistical analysis shows no correlation between school attendance at case closure and cost of intervention.

So what happened to the 60 pupils? There was a 33 per cent reduction in HoNOSCA measures for pupil symptoms and a similar change in HoNOSCA measures for parental understanding of their child and ability to use services effectively. There were distinct variations, with a few instances of marked deterioration or no change, and others of very substantial positive change.

Outcomes

The attendance of almost half the pupils improved by an additional 25 per cent or more, with eight pupils who had not been attending school at all, having established 100 per cent attendance at case closure. In six cases, the work undertaken enabled a judgement to be made that the picture was one of 'won't go' rather than 'can't go', and court action was undertaken by the Education Welfare Service.

Problems

The visions, objectives and intended methods of the project were clinically informed. However, insufficient time was allocated to embed this thinking at the outset. Later attempts to remedy the situation – not unnaturally – met with resistance.

The service was established at a time when dedicated Education Welfare time could not be allocated. This left a gap in the first two years, despite the commitment of individual officers who referred pupils.

Perceived pressure to be seen to be supporting schools (combined with the grant-funding arrangements) paradoxically may have reduced support by encouraging the service to take on more pupils than intended and reducing the intensity of their involvement.

The same pressure resulted in comprehensive and rigorous evaluation systems and procedures not being in place at the outset. Although remedied to an extent, time constraints continue to limit the provision of assessment and consultation that can be dedicated to the service by educational psychologists. Clinical psychology is not available at the time of writing.

It takes time for any new service to establish ways of working, and for other professionals to understand the resource that has become available. Once this stage was passed, the service was in danger of being overwhelmed: CAMHS identified pupils not previously known to support services; panels began to refer cases to the service routinely; and hospitals, doctors and parents became aware of the provision. Although staff became more rigorous in applying criteria for referral, they found it difficult to make appropriate cases wait.

Cases referred by panels were sometimes inappropriate, despite communication about the service through a variety of media, and overlap of personnel across panels.

The establishment of the service within a teaching support service resulted in most staff being on leave over school holidays. The long summer holiday, in particular, is a risk factor for the non-attendance of vulnerable children. While this was overcome, in part, by staff working in August on a good-will basis, a more robust structure is needed.

The skills that support staff bring have been beneficial and cost-effective. However, their conditions of service are such that notice periods are short. The sudden disruption of an important, habilitative relationship between worker and pupil has an adverse effect.

Drawing together thorough intervention programmes for pupils requires strong partnership working with local CAMHS, and is dependent on their capacity. The practice of some schools in taking pupils off roll when they have not attended for some time has prevented the service from working with some pupils.

The future

We hope that schools will seek support to assist their inclusion of potential school refusers and make referrals before patterns of non-attendance are too firmly established. One of the 'Freedoms and Flexibilities' granted through local Public Service Agreements in 2002 is that the Department of Education and Skills 'supports, if appropriate, the gradual re-integration into school of medically certified school phobics. Where this occurs, the days of attendance should be counted as present, and those of non-attendance as authorised absence'. While this protocol brings helpful clarity, and legitimises much current practice, it is unlikely to assist LEAs in overcoming the difficulties in establishing and addressing the nature and causes of non-attendance.

Considerable further work is needed to identify which pupils can be supported by which methods, so that resources may be targeted as effectively as possible. In the meantime, while 'bullying' may well be used by pupils as a catch-all for feelings of profound discomfort and unease about being in school, experience so far shows that this is an important area for schools to address to prevent unhappiness and non-attendance.

Total Support for Learning Project support activities

School – when the pupil is ready to return to school:

- transport to and from school;
- liaison with school staff including HoY, SENCO, tutors and class teachers;
- one-to-one in school but out of class;
- support in class;
- regular review meetings to ensure focus and progress is maintained.

Out of school – sometimes the young people are not ready for integration to school or school is not deemed appropriate and FE is sought:

- curriculum delivery at home;

- curriculum delivery at TSP base;
- Connexions involvement at base and at Connexions office;
- facilitating adult education courses for children out of school;
- facilitating entry and integration to FE college;
- facilitating other agency and voluntary service involvement;
- supporting attendance at specialist courses;
- setting up extended work-related learning opportunities.

Parents – often feel very pressured and are often on the receiving end of their child's behaviour as a result of their reluctance/refusal to attend school:

- providing a listening ear;
- giving direct advice;
- involving parents in decision-making;
- referral on to other services;
- providing group work with CAMHS or Social Services;
- helping build parental self-esteem through being positive.

Young people – it is important to involve the young person in their support. At the point of referral they often lack confidence, have low self-esteem and may be extremely anxious:

- listening to how they feel about things;
- building positive relationships and trust;
- setting targets and long-term goals;
- pacing the support to meet their needs, and not the needs of others;
- involving them in decision-making;
- undertaking confidence building activities, e.g. visiting crowded places;
- involving them in social activities including pottery, painting, bowling, falconry, community farms, tennis, internet café, walking, gardening;
- visiting places of local interest;
- teaching them strategies to help them feel less anxious;
- giving them the opportunity to meet other young people in a similar situation;
- being there for them.

6

Interagency working: the education of young people in public care

Marion Russell

Editors' introduction

Marion Russell considers the legislative requirements for supporting children in care. Children who are six to eight times more likely than the rest of the school population to have a Statement of Special Educational Needs. She emphasises the importance of teamwork across services, informed by accurate data-gathering and working in the context of corporate parental responsibility, where the challenge of advocacy and aspiration become part of the corporate professional role. Personal Education Plans are suggested as a mechanism for this endeavour, drawing together key people responsible for the child's wellbeing to contribute in a coherent manner.

Background

In May 2000 the government published the *Guidance on the Education of Young People in Public Care* jointly through the Departments of Health (DoH) and of Education and Skills (DfES 2002d), with new statutory duties for schools, LEAs and Social Services. This consolidated the government response to the reports and research of the previous decade. These reports examined the facts and the causes of poor educational achievement among the majority of children in care and their subsequent poor life chances. Statistics of educational attainment were worryingly low. Alongside the Guidance, the government has set targets for local authorities to raise educational attainment as shown by end-of-key-stage assessment and public examinations at 16-plus (DoH 2002b). Attainment for young people in public care is rising, but does not meet the targets set by government. In 2001, 50 per cent of Year 11 pupils in care achieved one GCSE/GNVQ or more, with newly published figures for 2002 rising to 53 per cent – compared to 95 per cent of the whole school population in both years. A matter of concern is that 42 per cent of Year 11 children in care were not entered for qualifications of this kind (DoH 2002b). Other statistics demonstrating the need for action can be found on the website.

Definition of children in public care

This group of children and young people is defined by the Children Act (1989) as those who are in the care of the local authority, either accommodated through a voluntary agreement with their parents or under a court order sharing parental responsibility with the local authority.

No distinction is made between these two definitions in the application of the Guidance; both are termed 'looked after' by the local authority and have equality under the new statutory duties of the Guidance. Looked After Children (LAC), Children in Public Care (CiPC), Young People in Public Care (YPiPC) and Children in Care (CiC) are terms used interchangeably in current literature.

The new corporate parent duties include: joint working and planning prior to moves of care placement or school; a Personal Education Plan drawn up within 20 school days of entering care or moving school; and Personal Education Plans reviewed as part of the statutory care plan review. The duties, however, are to be seen in the larger context of the responsibility of the corporate parent to:

- prioritise education;
- have high expectations of each child and young person;
- increase inclusion by changing and challenging attitudes;
- achieve continuity and stability;
- intervene early and make children in care a priority for action; and
- listen to children individually and in the joint messages they want to give to their corporate parents.

(DoH (2002b) Guidance: Sections 4.9–4.35)

SEN context

Children and young people in public care do not automatically have special educational needs by definition of being in care. Their abilities span those of the whole population. Many are capable of further and higher education and succeed when given appropriate opportunities. Many children in care do, however, have special educational needs. Some have missed schooling due to changes caused by their needs; and a significant number have emotional, social and behavioural difficulties. Children in public care are six to eight times more likely than the rest of the school population to have a Statement of Special Educational Needs.

How to move forward

The Guidance makes a clear statement to local authorities:

- Successful intervention cannot be achieved without a truly corporate effort – political ownership and leadership from senior management are essential;
- Much innovative and effective practice fails to become embedded in policy, practice and base funding because it is time limited and project-based;
- Factors contributing to the success of those who have been in care include:
    - stable and consistent care
    - early reading
    - regular school attendance
    - support from well informed foster carers
    - having a mentor
    - understanding the importance of education for future life chances, and
    - financial support for further and higher education.

(DoH (2002b) Section 2.16)

Lessons from research and practice suggest that, since 1999, the Standards Fund (DfES) and the Quality Protects Programme (DoH) in England have identified children and young people in public care as a target group, and offered a variety of ring-fenced funding streams to improve educational achievement. This has prompted a number of local authorities throughout England to create posts for this purpose, or redefine the work of existing educational teams for looked-after children. In 2000, the government also made an unprecedented move to support local authorities in England in the implementation of the Guidance, by creating the Education Protects Regional Implementation Advisers Team to run for twelve months. The team members were seconded one day a week from senior staff from local authority social services and education departments. All had evidence of sound practice but were also aware of the practicalities and the shortfalls in their own authorities and were able to support other local authorities in developing their understanding of the issues. Such has been the value of this support that at the time of writing the work of the Education Protects Team has been extended to March 2004. From 2004, Quality Protects funding will cease but the resources will be added to social services budgets, and authorities are expected to maintain the quality of provision. Standards Fund continues with looked-after children included in the overall allocation for vulnerable children. Similar funding has been allocated in Wales through Children First and GEST. Scotland and the Isle of Man are developing the focus on the education of children in care through their own legislative and funding programmes.

Corporate parenting

Children and young people are in care to the local authority, not to one department or service, and the whole local authority, therefore, has a legal and moral duty to act as a good parent. Historically, children in care have been perceived to be solely in the care of Social Services. This view continues to be expressed in the terminology used by some staff and in some documentation. It is important to challenge these perceptions and as the Guidance points out, 'the ways in which children in care are supported is a test of the effectiveness of the general policies and practice of a local authority' (DoH 2002b Section 1.5).

Many individuals are directly and indirectly involved in the practice of delivering corporate parenting. Schools have a key role, especially in developing inclusive ethos and practice. As collective groups have 'no memory', however, there must be a tool to record all plans and actions. For looked-after children this has been the LAC record system from DoH, but there is now a requirement for the education part of the statutory Care Plan to be fulfilled in the Personal Education Plan (PEP). The Personal Education Plan forms the long- and short-term planning to meet the child's current needs, however these needs arise. It incorporates all school plans, such as Individual Education Plans. The social worker, teachers and carers need to make their contribution. Together these people are the face-to-face contact of the corporate parent for the child. Birth parents, except under exceptional circumstances, contribute too. Crucially, as happens within families with good relationships and communication, the child or young person will also have a major input with their perceptions of what is needed, and just as importantly, of what is going well. Corporate parenting is not limited to the contributions of the social worker, carer and designated teacher in school. Housing departments, for example, should be looking at their standards for provision for care leavers. Libraries and leisure services can contribute significant services and opportunities for children of all abilities and interests in developing personal confidence, awareness, skills and interests. Recent research offers sound suggestions for practical corporate parenting action (Jackson *et al.* 2003).

Data gathering

For all authorities, accurate data systems are vital to good parenting. Most authorities have significant difficulty with this, as traditionally systems held in social services have been localised and are not suitable for the complexity of education information gathering required by new statutory returns and monitoring requirements. The most successful authorities are those that have reliable update systems and specific designated personnel to change entries promptly when children enter or leave care. The developments in LEA pupil data systems are channelling attention and resources into improved data collection and analysis. The new DfES requirement for PLASC (Pupil Level Annual School Census) to record children who are or have been looked after, and by which local authority, will increase the accuracy of cross-checking data. The government is also directing comprehensive data systems through the Integrated Children's System (ICS) for multiagency information on all children in contact with Social Services and the Information, Referral and Tracking (IRT) data system for vulnerable children. ICS is currently at a pilot stage in only three local authorities. In the meantime, the need to balance information sharing within and across agencies, while maintaining confidentiality within the Data Protection Act and other professional requirements, is exercising these agencies considerably.

Personal Education Plans

Personal Education Plans can be seen as the record of the level of planning that good parents make, often subconsciously, for their children's education. Many parents plan well in advance for the school placement they want, provide suitable study facilities for older children, expect to hear reading daily with younger pupils, and ensure good communication with school staff over illness, general progress in school, family disruption, celebrations or events which affect the child. If this is important for children with relative stability, how much more so for those whose life has known – and may well still be experiencing – significant turbulence and broken relationships? When completed and used well, the Personal Education Plan works as an effective tool to draw together all the key people responsible for the child's wellbeing, and allows each individual, including the child, to contribute. This ensures that no area is neglected and gives a perspective on the wider issues that parents give, including the encouragement of aspirations and praise for regular small achievements. It allows early intervention and planning for known and understandable difficulties, such as those which the child has experienced, or will experience, during periods of uncertainty and change. It also brings cohesion to school action for special educational needs, alternative curricula and mental health needs in a context that gives a sound overview for everyone. Good long-term planning also incorporates the practicalities of planning for the child's future schooling at transition between phases and also education beyond statutory school age. Without this exchange of information and planning, pupils are placed in a vulnerable position. The emotional effects of practical events, such as failed instances of contact with birth parents, the strain of legal proceedings and change of care placement, can all lead to explosive or withdrawn types of behaviour. These types of behaviour, where not understood or put in context by the school, have, in numerous cases, led to exclusions, which further alienate the child from the long-term advantages of education.

Advocacy and co-operation

Some thought needs to be given here to the principle of advocacy. Most parents advocate for their children; but whereas it is part of parental instinct to seek the best to meet one's children's needs, it is more difficult for professionals to have the long-term knowledge, understanding and passion of a parent. Designated teachers are required to be advocates within the schools, but in many schools the designated teacher is a member of senior management. Others have pastoral responsibilities for the whole school, and advocacy fits well with this. Many will sense conflict with their perceived role within senior management, which requires that the needs of all pupils be met, especially regarding sound discipline in school. Schools with good inclusive practice readily grasp the practical and emotional implications of the difficulties experienced by children in public care and seek to extend the necessary additional care or structures. Finally, at its heart, good corporate parenting is inclusive practice working effectively for each child.

How corporate parenting has developed in Lancashire

Involvement

Lancashire is a large county with a wide socioeconomic range across diverse rural and urban areas, and ethnic diversity. There are approximately 1,300 children in care at any one time. The first priority was to develop the corporate response based on the national guidance. In 2001, the Authority established an interdepartmental Steering Group covering both Social Services (SSD) and

Education and Cultural Services (ECSD) Directorates. The Steering Group currently comprises: the County Council portfolio holder for Children and Families; the County Education Welfare Officer; the Quality and Review Manager; the multiagency policy officer; a social services area manager and a team manager; an adviser from the School Effectiveness Service; and the members of the Education of Looked After Children (ELAC) Team. The composition of the Group is under review and will need to be extended to include representatives from schools and the health authorities.

Supportive policy and practical guidance

One of the first tasks of the Steering Group was to produce 'Guidance Notes on the Education of Children and Young People in Public Care' for schools, social workers and other professionals in August 2001. This was followed up initially through the provision of joint training for designated teachers and social workers. The new document provides clear procedures for the Personal Education Plan and other educational action by setting out good professional practice and defining responsibilities for social workers, designated teachers and carers. Action Lists provide information on the most common situations to be met, e.g. the actions to be taken when a child comes into care or ceases to be in care. These are set out in a readily accessible form, supported by detail within the PEP.

Education of Looked After Children Team

The Steering Group also created the structure for a small ELAC Team to assist the development of specific supportive action to change practice and to identify further needs. The Team comprises a Personal Education Plan Co-ordinator with a teaching background and two ELAC Support Officers, respectively with LEA and Social Services backgrounds. The Team is jointly funded by the LEA and social services, and works to a joint business plan, which has a remit across both directorates.

The concept of the whole authority as corporate parent has remained prominent in Lancashire and the vision remains that looked-after children should be a priority group across all services. The Authority aims to recognise the existing skills within social work teams, schools and LEA services and to build the understanding of looked-after children through supportive action. The ELAC Team can be seen as a catalyst, bringing about joint action where communication previously did not exist, and identifying areas of working which did not include looked-after children, or even, perhaps unknowingly, discriminated against them through unsympathetic working practices. The Team also offers multiagency contact through localised network meetings and training.

Personal Education Plans

The Personal Education Plan is developing in Lancashire as a tool for pupil level corporate parenting work, as it involves the children and the key people around them in practical day-to-day action. Committed members of staff are seeing the benefits of developing the PEP in this way and indicate that good planning will provide early intervention. In a large authority, however, it is not a straightforward task to ensure development of good practice across widely differing socioeconomic and geographical areas. Reviewing Officers (Independent chairs of Looking After Children Review meetings) are helpful in developing consistency regarding PEPs. They report mixtures of good practice and the need for further developmental work across the county. Current requests for advice and support indicate gaps in the social workers' understanding of education systems and weaknesses in the schools' and LEA services' appreciation of the rigour needed to support children in care effectively when life is traumatic. The model of what good parents do for their children is helpful and leads to interesting debate.

Experience of good practice in using PEPs is emerging to show these benefits: that designated teachers feel much more helpfully informed of the child's situation and needs, social workers understand more about the education processes and carers find their roles and skills more valued. The involvement of the child is helping to reinforce the good practice advocated in the 2002 SEN Code of Practice and already established in the principles of the Children Act (1989). The multiagency involvement in this process is encouraging greater understanding of the child's perspective.

Longer-term changes towards corporate parenting

The corporate parenting theme is slowly developing through Lancashire and includes the following long-term developments:

• Advisers in the School Effectiveness Service will, in their autumn statutory visits, ask routinely about the numbers of looked-after children on roll, the incidence of Personal Education Plans, the effectiveness of these plans and any strategic issues.

- The Educational Psychology Area Services all have a designated psychologist with particular responsibility for raising and resolving LAC issues.
- Work is under way to identify a designated member of each LEA County and Area Service and each Social Services Children and Families Team to act as lead person for education of looked-after children matters. Current SEN/EPS work on seeking the pupil's views for Statement reviews is contributing to the work on developing a pupil-centred perspective in the Personal Education Plan.
- School Admission Appeals Panels have received training and are developing a protocol to support planning of school placement prior to placement move, when appeals for school places are needed.
- Detailed procedures have been drawn up to support social workers, designated teachers and carers in defining responsibility and accessing the full range of education services for pupils in early years settings and schools.
- Liaison is taking place with the Early Years Teacher Teams and Area SENCOs to offer support to non-maintained early years settings.
- The PEP has been developed with current national and local assessment systems in mind, including options for P Scales and Lancashire PIVATS system for pupils with special educational needs.
- The PIVATS system will be encouraged as an effective means of identifying the needs of pupils who have emotional, social and behavioural difficulties and who may also be of average and above average ability.
- The concept and practicalities of corporate parenting are being explored in the context of multiagency locality groups within the county.
- Reviewing Officers nominate children from each month's reviews for the efforts they have made to maintain or improve their educational progress – progress which may not necessarily be measurable in conventional attainment terms – such as attendance at school during times of personal difficulty or improvements in attitude to making good relationships with peers.
- The Leader of the Council sends a card and gift token to each child nominated that month, with an invitation following for a presentation event for all those who have received an award over the quarter.
- Listening to children is another theme of corporate parenting. The Children and Young People's Panel meets with county councillors, policy officers and the Lancashire Children's Rights Service. The Panel is represented on the Quality Protects Panel, which then addresses practical and policy matters that affect young people's lives.
- Lancashire Education and Cultural Services and Social Services Directorates are working to create a protocol and joint practice for inspection of care

standards and educational standards for Out of County Placements for children with Statements of SEN.

- Further joint working is being explored to create LEA input to placement planning decisions for residential placements with education on-site for children without Statements of SEN.
- Private residential schools and homes with education on-site are being offered opportunities to access LEA training and professional development for national strategies through the School Standards Service.

Other short-term initiatives have also been implemented in Lancashire and in many authorities across England. Good examples can be found on the Education Protects website. These are helpful, but true corporate parenting begins only when such proven actions find their place in long-term funding and changes in policy and practice that best suit local need. There is now a consistent focus on children in care in current national developments (e.g. School Admissions Code of Practice to be implemented from September 2004; *Every Child Matters* Green Paper, July 2003). We also await with interest the long-term benefits in legislative and conceptual consistency as a result of the move of children and families services from DoH to DfES in June 2003.

Conclusion

Where good practice is established, schools are likely to be fulfilling most of the requirements of the Personal Education Plan. Some schools are also seeing it as a useful tool for pupils in need of multiagency input, whether or not in care. Similarly, the education issues that arise for looked-after children support other multiagency working to improve services in a child-focused way. Where individuals at a day-to-day level and at strategic middle and higher management level are committed to the needs of all children, the needs of children in care are most effectively advocated and met. Research, government restructuring and national initiatives offer many challenges. Immense satisfaction can be derived, however, from seeing hard work and creative thinking result in individual children's educational opportunities increased to match their peers, and their life chances improved.

Editors' introduction to Chapters 7 and 8

The chapters by Ann Butt and Claire Cosser, and Gill Dixon and Naresh Gahir, on supporting transition offer important insights into support work through well-focused examples of materials used from early years settings to school, and primary to secondary phases. Most LEAs would recognise these as significant periods of increase in requests for statutory assessment and as these chapters demonstrate, good support at this level, even if only short-term, can significantly reduce the anxieties of parents, children and schools. The examples given are poignant in that they deal with two groups of children increasing in numbers and to which there has been much national debate, i.e. emotional and behavioural difficulties and autistic spectrum disorders.

Butt and Cosser demonstrate the importance of positive assessment as a significant aspect of their approach to a proactive and whole-school project. This creates a structure that enables and enskills others, including parents, through which they are able to resist the development of a dependency culture by 'giving away' their expertise to those closest to the child. A significant aspect of this approach is the innovative way in which they articulate the voice of the child. They provide many good examples of practical materials and approaches.

Dixon and Gahir demonstrate how effective an LEA support service can be when its work is well targeted and based on short-term projects. Transition of pupils with behaviour needs from primary to secondary is a major concern nationally, but this chapter demonstrates how a small amount of resource effectively deployed and carefully evaluated can produce big results. As with Butt and Cosser, the work is proactive and specifically aims to reduce school dependency. Until such time as schools can work more collaboratively across phases it will be important that services such as those described identify pupil need and act to ensure support. The overall aim is to build pupil resilience, and as with Butt and Cosser, the practical materials devised prove to be an effective 'passport' to inclusion.

7

Supporting transition: preschool setting into first placement

Ann Butt and Claire Cosser

This chapter describes the transition policies and procedures of Derby City Special Educational Needs Support Service (SENSS) for children who have an identified special need and who have received preschool support moving into their first placement in a maintained setting. This may be a nursery class, nursery school or reception class, but the procedures essentially remain the same. It attempts to explain the essential features of the transition process and how these have developed.

Derby City became a unitary authority in 1997 after previously being part of, and administered by, Derbyshire. The Derby City Special Educational Needs Support Service (SENSS) was created in 1998 by the amalgamation of the inherited separate support services into one large service. The preschool staff are placed within the sensory and preschool team. Children with sensory difficulties tend to be supported by teachers who are specialists in a specific area, although there is some joint working. Preschool staff numbers have risen from one teacher, when the service was created, to the present levels of one teacher and three full-time-equivalent support workers, which has greatly increased the numbers of children who can receive regular support, and has also developed the range and quality of areas such as transition. All of the children who receive support are referred through a multiagency assessment and referral panel and have moderate to severe needs in more than one area of development. They are supported until they enter statutory provision, at either nursery or school age.

The transition procedures described in this chapter have evolved gradually with many revisions, until reaching their current format. They continue to be evaluated on a regular basis and respond as much as possible to the needs of individual children, their families and settings.

For many parents of children with additional needs transition between any provision is difficult and can be distressing. The transition into the first setting is the most frightening of all. It was vital, therefore, to develop transition processes which increased parental confidence, gave them a degree of control over the process and provided them with a medium through which they could tell people all the small important things about their child – getting professionals to look beyond the diagnosis and to see their child as an individual from day one. This is particularly evident with children with communication difficulties where parents' worries centre around their child not being able to make their needs known to unfamiliar adults, with their attempts at expression being misinterpreted.

When the Special Educational Needs Support Service was created, existing staffing levels at that time only allowed for monthly visits, and transition procedures were limited. Core practice usually involved a written report for the setting by the advisory teacher and a meeting with the teacher, parents and setting, in addition to usual school arrangements. The gradual increase in staffing allowed an increase in the frequency of visits and a consequent clearer view of parental perspectives. Parents were much more willing and able to talk about their needs and fears and the needs of their children when there was a closer working relationship, established within a framework of more frequent visits to the home.

Parents' concerns around their child beginning their first placement obviously vary enormously, but often centre around worries that people will not understand the trigger points of distress or respond positively to their communicative behaviour and play. Increasingly, we were having children referred to the service with significant and complex needs regarding their communication, social and early play skills. These children often find transition into new settings difficult and benefit from a range of visits with a familiar adult. Photographs that can be discussed with carers at home can reinforce this. It was with this knowledge that we examined our transition policy and associated practices and found them to be lacking in several key areas. First, in preparing the child for the setting; second, in allowing the parents a voice to share vital information about their child, that only they can provide; and, finally, to provide the parent with resources and a method to enable them to pass this information on.

The model that has developed has six key elements:
- photo book for the child;
- development of personal passport in conjunction with parent and support worker;
- a transition report with a newly agreed format;
- preparation for the setting, including training and provision of resources;
- passing on a continuous assessment profile, which spans preschool and Foundation stage; and
- visits to the setting with parent and child.

Photo books

Photo books of settings are used extensively and for a range of different purposes according to the needs of the child. For a child with significant communication difficulties or autistic spectrum disorder, the books are used to familiarise a child with a setting before they make their first visit. The child is then able to match key areas and people to their book, which can be looked at repeatedly. This sharing can be reinforced by the use of signs and symbols as necessary. For other children the book would act as a memory prompt, and repeated access to this information would allow them to assimilate and remember the information, as many children rely heavily on visual learning. The book also gives opportunities for those parents or siblings who are unable to accompany the child on the visit of a share in the experience of getting to know their new school.

The books have been very successful and evaluation from the parents shows them being highlighted as one of the most significant elements of the transition process for their children.

A child with autistic spectrum disorder had spent several days sharing his book with his family who had been telling him simply what he would do when he went to school. He was a child who found new environments difficult and yet he approached the school confidently, recognised his class teacher from her photograph in the book and surprised everyone by saying 'Hello, Mrs X, are you going to teach me my letters and numbers?' The book also proved to be a useful discussion tool, so that he could tell his family what had happened at school using the pictures as a prompt.

Personal passports

Personal passports were not a new medium, but until recently had never been used within SENSS for transition. The term is accredited to Sally Millar (1995) at the Call Centre in Edinburgh who described them as

> a collection of important and well-presented information about an individual with sensory and communication difficulties, who cannot speak for themselves, for the purpose of facilitating communication and understanding.

With reference to work in our Derby team an apt description is: 'A written way of parents passing on important information about their child to an individual or setting.' While the focus of their use has been on supporting transition into the child's first placement, they have also been used as a practical tool to aid inclusion and access to the full range of early play and social activities such as playgroups, creches, holiday activities, respite and childcare situations.

One of the most important features of the passports developed with families in Derby has been that they are created in the style of presentation that parents choose. They have often taken the form of:

- simple notebook approach with photos of child, families and activities;
- laminated spiral-bound book, purpose-made to meet the wishes and requirements of families;
- small pocket photo albums with text and photos inserted in ready-made pockets; and
- photocopied 'handout'-type sheets.

Within the Derby model, rather than a professional leading the process and inviting parents to add their own comments, the whole process has been driven by the parents' own agenda as to what the passport should contain and how it should be presented. Headings from these 'family focused passports' have often included:

- My name is (title page)
- Important things about me
- Family and friends
- Things that make me happy and how I show you
- Things that may upset or frighten me and how I show you
- What I need to help me understand what you are saying
- Systems of communication
- Things I am learning to do by myself
- Things that are rewards for me.

Some extracts from personal passports are included here with parental permission.

Important things about me

If you play with me I can enjoy lots of different activities – cars, books, balls, farm and zoo animals – but if I am left by myself I often tap with a toy or stick or start spinning a circle. I may also want something to spin or tap if I am tired or upset – Mum and Dad usually let me have something like this at these times to comfort

me, but the rest of the time try and tempt me with more interesting things to do!
(Andrew, a boy aged 4 with Down's syndrome. Written on transition into reception class.)

Things I like and how I show you

I show that I like something by wrinkling up my eyes, I really like it if you do this back to me. I sometimes put my fingers in my ears when I am happy. I sometimes make noises when I'm happy, this is usually a high-pitched sound.
(Dean, aged 4, with autistic spectrum disorder. Written on transition into nursery class.)

Things I don't like and how I show you

I don't like new situations and I need time to get used to the new routine. This may take me a few weeks. I don't like busy situations and lots of children, or a new person entering the room. When I am unsure, I may put my head down or lower my gaze. I may put my hand over my head and say 'I frightened'. I may repeat myself or I may refuse to co-operate.
(Martin, aged 4, with a language disorder. Written on transition into reception class.)

Important things about me

I am a very sociable little girl with family and friends that I know well, but often very shy with unfamiliar people and situations. Certain noises and actions (especially crying and screaming) can upset me. I won't cry loudly but I'm likely to bury my head and sob quietly, so you might not realise that I am actually crying.
(Shabana, aged 3, with Down's syndrome. Written on transition into nursery school.)

Playing with other children

I am learning how to share and take turns but I will probably need you to remind me lots of times. Sometimes I do push and I need you to remind me that I must not do this. I do understand 'no', and if I am doing something that I shouldn't, please just sign and firmly say 'no'.
(Zak, aged 5, with learning difficulties. Written on transition into reception class in enhanced resource infant school.)

As with the above examples, and in line with Millar's original work, passports are usually written in the first person; this seems appropriate for a number of reasons.

- It makes the author of the passport consider very carefully the child's perspective and is very much about using the words that the child would use themselves if they were able to.
- It presents the reader with a very personal account and, therefore, hopefully, triggers a sensitive and individual response.
- It presents the voice of an individual child rather than simply describing the expected traits of a condition or syndrome.

Passports are written during home visits, by parents working with a support worker or teacher, who usually takes responsibility for the organisation of necessary resources and their production. This professional support in helping a family produce a passport is essential. If professionals just talk about a passport as a good idea but leave the family to produce it, it often increases the feelings of guilt and stress within a family as it becomes yet another task which they are too busy to comprehend or complete. As we firmly believe that this is a vital tool within our transition procedures its importance needs to be recognised in the high quality and care of presentation and resources used.

Parents own the passport and are always provided with two copies, one for them to keep and use as appropriate and one to give to the setting. It is important that the parent chooses the context and timing at which they pass it on to the setting. Passports are not handed over by support staff. Some parents give permission for their passports to be shared with others, which gives parents ideas and a clear picture of what they might be aiming for.

Transition report

The original transition report, which was in use as the service developed, contained descriptions of the nature of a child's difficulties and their needs. It also contained a summary of the type of support that a child had received, and sometimes a profile of skills was attached, but this was not common practice or formal policy. Although we initially used this format, we were conscious that it concentrated on the deficit model of the child and did not identify skills, strengths and talents or describe what the child could do. Without an accurate description of the child's current skills, it is impossible to provide the next appropriate stage of their learning experience. An example of this is: a statement that 'a child is not yet toilet-trained' does not indicate whether the child has any understanding of being wet, indicates to an adult that they need to go to the toilet or sometimes take themselves to the toilet. It is therefore difficult for a receiving setting to plan and provide experiences and resources.

The report was reviewed about two years ago and the format adapted to take into account some of the difficulties highlighted. This aimed to give precise descriptors of a child's current skills and needs, as well as an overall picture of a child's interests, strengths and response to adult interventions and strategies. An assessment profile, along with the current IEP or play plan and sample recent visit notes, in addition to the report, now constitute a package of information passed on to settings. This is a consistent package provided by any member of the team in line with the transition policy.

We have consulted with the settings who have experienced the most recent transitions about the usefulness of the report. The consultations were generally positive, but inevitably there were some ideas for change. The requests for change included more information about the rate of the child's progress and their pattern of development from birth, if the information is available to us. There were also requests to give more information about family background and more detailed medical information from those agencies involved with the child. The transition report is currently being amended in the light of these suggestions and will be piloted with the transitions at the end of the summer term.

Transition reports were initially sent out immediately after the child had transferred and may or may not have been accompanied by a visit to the setting by the teacher. This was mainly owing to lack of time and large caseloads. We now aim to have a consistent model of policy and practice where a meeting is held between SENSS, the setting and parents, where the transition report is discussed and its implications for the child and the setting highlighted. The meeting is timed in consultation with the setting and is the formal handing-over after a series of transition visits.

Staff training

Children with very specific conditions need staff that understand their needs and have sufficient knowledge to feel confident in providing for them. Staff training on specific issues is always offered to settings and may be carried out by members of the preschool team or teachers who are skilled in specific areas such as visual, hearing or physical impairment, autistic spectrum disorder or communication difficulties. Schools are encouraged to consider training for their staff, and are also encouraged to involve as many school staff as possible including midday supervisors and school secretaries, who will have dealings with the child and should understand their difficulties. Sometimes parents wish to be involved in this training and some like to provide input about their child in conjunction with the specific information about a condition given by the teacher. This training often takes place in a staff meeting and can be followed up by further sessions at a later date as necessary.

Staff may also need help and advice on producing specific resources to work with a child. Visual timetables, for example, are often produced for settings in the first instance as experience has shown that people are more likely to use a technique which is new to them, if they are provided with resources. If people are unsure about the efficacy of something, they are unlikely to invest the time in researching and making it. Advice on specific resource needs is also given as appropriate.

Assessment profile

Each child who receives support from the team has a developmental profile completed as an ongoing record of skills and progress. The choice of profile is dependent on their level of need and the type of support received. The team offers Portage to parents, and the children who receive this will have the Portage developmental profile completed. The children who have very significant levels of need usually have the Pathways profile completed. Most of the other children will have the Ann Locke Teaching Talking profiles completed. These profiles give a clear indication of a child's needs and areas of relative strength and show the progress made over a period of time. They follow the child, and are part of the package of information passed to settings at point of transition. Parents are often offered copies of them to keep, and sometimes to complete, as an ongoing record.

Visits

Visits are vital to many children to enable them to adapt to being in a new setting. Similarly, they provide settings with an opportunity to plan and adapt to meet the needs of children who are about to be admitted. The nature, number and timing of these will vary according to the needs of the child. Some children will need a step-by-step approach to familiarisation with each part of the new environment – visits to an empty classroom, meeting one key member of staff, progressing to taking part in one aspect of the class routine and, ultimately, joining in a whole-class activity. Visits are always accompanied by support staff and parents and are alongside the usual home visiting, which remains until the child is admitted onto the school roll.

Some children need a more carefully structured visit, and liaison with the school is vital to achieve this. A strip containing a timetable of activities which the child can remove as they are completed, often allays anxiety for children with communication difficulties, although it is vital that staff keep to the agreed order of activities.

For parents, the visits allow them to build confidence in the school's abilities to respond to their child's needs and confidence in their child being able to cope with the new setting. It also provides the parents several occasions when they can pass on information to staff rather than relying on one formal meeting.

Evaluation

The transition process has recently been evaluated by parents whose children have just accessed their first placement and have received support from the service. Parents were asked to comment on what the most useful aspect of the transition process was for their child and for themselves. They were also given the opportunity to make suggestions for improvement if necessary. Below is a selection of the comments received:

> *Geoffrey is now enjoying school and is relaxed in his environment because of the knowledge he gained by the visits and the school book and the support from preschool staff.*

> *Having the photos was good because Joshua could familiarise himself with school and when he visited it wasn't a totally strange experience. This has been proved, as Joshua has settled into school and is really enjoying it.*

The parents nearly all highlighted the writing of the personal passports as the most useful part of the process for them. A parent summed up this feeling by writing:

> *The most important part for me was the personal passport because it made me less worried about anyone not knowing what Colin is like; his likes and dislikes. Now the school has this they will know everything they need to know about him.*

The comments made in the evaluation were all positive about the process and the support that had been received. There were no suggestions for improvement.

The SENSS preschool and sensory team has developed its procedures for transition but is not complacent. We are still conscious that there are areas to be considered and further improved. Our current concern is the need for a joint meeting to plan for each child's transition, which does not always happen. Our aim is to include parents, SENSS, school/nursery and the Educational Psychology Service, but our difficulty lies in the timing of this; too often the confirmation of school placement and resources are too late for this to happen. Our vision is to plan the whole transition four to six weeks before it takes place so that everyone is clear about what will happen, when it will happen and who is responsible for what. We are working to achieve this, not only to improve services for children but also to improve the confidence of parents in placements and the confidence of placements to deal with an increasingly wide range of additional needs.

No system is ever perfect, but the current procedures are giving children the best transition into first placement that we are able to give with our current resources. There is no doubt that initiatives, both on a national and local basis, will continue to challenge us to adapt and improve, and this is what we will endeavour to do.

8

Supporting transition: from primary to secondary school

Gill Dixon and Naresh Gahir

In 2002, the Warwickshire Learning and Behaviour Support Service ran a small-scale project to support the transition of pupils with statements for emotional and behavioural difficulties from Key Stage 2 to Key Stage 3. This is a brief outline of the project and its results.

Background

The Warwickshire Learning and Behaviour Support Service (LABSS) works principally in Warwickshire schools on an annual subscription basis with pupils at School Action (SEN Code) who have either learning and/or behaviour difficulties. LABSS operates as an independent business unit within the LEA, with funding for pupils at School Action and School Action Plus for EBD and learning difficulties delegated to the county schools.

On a day-to-day basis we work directly with individual pupils, small groups or classes of pupils, advise and support teachers, and provide training for staff in individual schools, and more widely. Many schools use LABSS in a consultancy role in relation to individual pupils or whole-school SEN issues and policy development. A more recent focus for LABSS has been the negotiation with Griffith University in Australia to market one of its programmes known as 'Friends' as a national initiative in the UK.

Different divisions and sections within Warwickshire Education Department also have subscription arrangements or commissions with LABSS to help them fulfil their obligations in supporting schools. One of these annual subscriptions is bought by the Assessment, Statement and Review Service (ASRS) to provide support for individual pupils with statements on a short–term project basis. The priorities for support are agreed by the members of the ASRS team and communicated to the area manager of LABSS who allocates resources, liaises with the school and manages and supervises staff. Support is usually a Special Educational Needs Assistant (SEA) within the class and teacher support on a consultancy basis from EBD specialists.

The Warwickshire ASRS team identified a concern that, historically, a number of pupils with EBD statements failed to transfer successfully to secondary schools and had been excluded within a year of transfer. In the previous year, during the summer term, the ASRS team prioritised three pupils who were transferring to secondary school with statements for EBD. All three pupils transferred successfully with LABSS support, and at the time of writing are still included in the same mainstream secondary schools. The ASRS team requested that this pilot project be extended to a larger number of pupils. They specified that the support offered should be short-term, additional to the statement funding and be designed to promote empowerment rather than dependency in the receiving schools.

Rationale behind our approach

Why do pupils with a high level of emotional and behavioural difficulties fail on transfer to secondary after being included in their primary schools? Possible hypotheses about causes could include: the move to a less child-centred environment and a greater focus in Key Stage 3 on delivering the curriculum, rather than differentiating for differing needs, leading to a deficit view of the pupil. Organisational factors might include: the lack of an accessible consistent mentor/key person; the additional stressors of changing classrooms, moving around a larger campus and adjusting to new expectations and differing teacher styles. Most pupils presenting with behavioural difficulties also have associated emotional difficulties and there is ample research evidence to suggest that disaffection significantly interferes with a child's ability to handle even the ordinary pressures of everyday life. For the child struggling with feelings of fear, sadness, apprehension, worthlessness or guilt, coping with daily routine is hard, let alone accessing and achieving within the National Curriculum. The additional stress associated with a major life change can be the trigger to a crisis and to behavioural difficulties.

All pupils with EBD tend to have learning deficits of problem-solving and positive coping skills. They characteristically have 'negative self-talk habits' and 'unrealistic self-valuation'. They tend to be biased towards a tendency to interpret or perceive threat in ambiguous situations. *Bright Futures*, the report from the Mental Health Foundation (1999), identifies risk factors for mental health in the child including: being a boy; having low IQ and learning disability;

specific developmental delay; communication difficulty; difficult temperament; illness; academic failure; and low self-esteem. Most of our target pupils fitted this profile.

Primary school teachers may have more time and opportunity to establish and build a relationship with each pupil, so it is perhaps easier for them to regard pupils with challenging behaviour as an individual with emotional development needs rather than a personal threat to their teaching and authority. In primary schools, statemented funding seems more likely to be channelled directly into funds for a person to support the individual pupil. In secondary schools, support may be targeted on groups or curriculum areas. We feel it is desirable to empower secondary teachers to take a more proactive view of these pupils and to put in place measures to build resilience against emotional difficulties and encourage pupils to take responsibility for behaviour.

> Resilience seems to involve several elements. Firstly, a sense of self-esteem and self-confidence; secondly, a belief in one's own self-efficacy and ability to deal with change and adaptation; and thirdly, a repertoire of social problem-solving approaches. (DfES 2001c :10)

Process

In the summer of 2002, the ASRS team requested that the transition project be extended across all four areas of Warwickshire. The aim was to produce a model of excellence for use within Warwickshire schools that could support the successful transition of identified primary pupils with high-level behaviour difficulties into secondary schools. Warwickshire is a county that actively promotes the inclusion of pupils with EBD in primary mainstream schools and there are no EBD special schools for the primary phase.

The project was co-ordinated by an EBD specialist support teacher, and hands-on work with the pupils undertaken by three SEAs. The total SEA time available was less than 2 f.t.e.

The Primary Phase of the project, lasting three weeks, started on 1 July 2002. The secondary phase, eight weeks in duration, ran from September to October 2002. Seven statemented pupils were supported.

Procedures: Primary Phase

The Project Co-ordinator made contact with each primary school via the school SENCO and an initial meeting with SENCO, classroom teacher, and, where possible, classroom assistant of the identified pupils was arranged. Schools were asked to provide copies of any relevant information such as behaviour programmes, IEPs and statements for the Project Co-ordinator.

The purpose of the initial meeting with primary school staff was to elicit useful information that could then be summarised and presented to key staff in secondary schools. As the following demonstrates:

Warwickshire Transition Project (Year 6 to Year 7)

Aim: To support the successful transition of identified pupils, with high-level behaviour difficulties, into secondary schools.

Pupil: K..... Smith

Primary School:

Secondary School:

Meeting with Mrs B. SENCO at   Junior School on Wednesday 3 July 2002

Background Information

1. K..... is mildly colour blind and has a Statement for SpLD.

2. Behaviour has been a big cause for concern throughout school and various behaviour programmes have been used to support K....., with varying degrees of success. He has needed considerable SEA support, not always for learning but often for pastoral care.

3. Some of K.....'s behaviours have included: calling out in class, hurting other children and refusing to do work. They could be attention seeking behaviours. There does not seem to be a consistent trigger.

4. K..... has a current IEP on which a target is to accept SEA support for learning. He is accepting support more now and he prefers pre-teaching sessions, where work is explained to him by the SEA beforehand, so that in class he can work more independently.

5. K..... finds change difficult. He takes time to settle into school after he has had a holiday.

6. Mrs B. feels that K..... has low self-esteem and lacks confidence in reading and writing.

Positive Behaviours and Progress

1. K..... is able to accept support more often now.
2. He has started to complete tasks in class.
3. He does have the ability to learn.
4. He is good with computers.
5. He is good at football and sometimes plays for the school team.
6. Mr T. D., K.....'s class teacher, said that K..... is a very able middle distance runner and has great potential for sustained running. He said that K..... has: 'natural ability for running that could be developed.'
7. K..... has a good sense of humour and can be easy going and amiable.
8. There are bigger gaps between anger outbursts which is positive.
9. K...... shows good understanding in science and his concentration has improved.
10. In class, he is able to follow class rules, co-operate with others and is much better at not resenting being told what to do.

Support for K.... Smith at B.R.C. Secondary School

1. Mrs B. and Mr D. feel that K..... will need the following to help him succeed at his new school:
    - clear structure with clear boundaries and rules;
    - may need work on anger management;
    - will need an adult who he can make a relationship with and talk to should he need pastoral support;
    - is far more receptive to school programmes when mum is involved;
    - will need consistency from ALL staff in a structured environment.

Initial interview with K.....Smith

1. K..... is anxious about moving up to his secondary school because he does not know anyone.
2. He would find it useful to have somewhere he can go in order to calm down, should the need arise, along with a teacher he can talk to.
3. He likes to have rewards for work.
4. He would like to sit near pupils who are quite quiet and sensible and finds it off-putting when he sits near pupils who are chatty and noisy.
5. He really enjoys cooking and likes running.

6. He would really like mum to be invited to school to hear positive things about him instead of negative things.

During the Primary Phase of the Transition Project, the Project Co-ordinator had either one or two meetings with each pupil at their primary school, and in two instances was also able to observe and meet with pupils on Induction Day at their secondary school. The information that pupils provided was summarised and later shared with key staff, notably SENCOs, year heads and form tutors at the secondary schools.

In pupil meetings, a range of techniques was used to elicit information and to focus on how pupils can take responsibility for their behaviour and learning. These techniques included basic counselling skills, i.e. active listening, role play and Solution Focused Brief Therapy.

Where possible, further meetings were set up at the primary schools to which SENCOs of secondary schools and parents or carers were invited to meet with primary school staff. Where such meetings did not occur, the Project Co-ordinator made visits to secondary schools to meet SENCOs and, where possible, other key staff, for example form tutors, year heads or behaviour co-ordinators within those secondary schools. The purpose of these meetings was to pass on relevant information from primary school staff, pupils and carers, and to discuss LABSS support and school support staff for the pupil at the start of the autumn term.

Procedures: Secondary Phase

After LABSS SEA support had been negotiated with schools, the Project Co-ordinator liaised with LABSS SEAs to discuss the nature of support to be offered. It was agreed that SEAs would work with school staff to endeavour to create a supportive, secure environment for pupils. Responsibilities of SEAs varied from school to school, but generally included the following:

- provision of in-class support, not only for the identified pupil but also for other pupils in class:
- advice and guidance to pupils about making appropriate behaviour choices;
- modelling of appropriate behaviour management strategies including a high level of positive behaviour and learning-specific encouragement to pupils;
- key link between all parties and giving professional advice to the Project Co-ordinator and school staff about the needs of the pupil;

- structured observations of pupils in the form of tracking positive performance in attitude, learning and conduct behaviour in lessons. These observations were typed up and copies given to SENCOs to be disseminated to key staff in each school.

The aim of tracking positive performance was to:

- identify positive behaviours that the pupil demonstrated in terms of attitude, learning, conduct and relationship with others;
- feed back to the pupil specific concrete examples of positive performance and therefore build learner esteem;
- use the information to feed back to parents/carers and school staff appropriate behaviours the pupil engaged in, so as to avoid unhelpful 'labelling' of the pupil.

Tracking positive performance was done regularly for the duration of the Secondary Phase of the Transition Project. Where schools had little or no LABSS SEA support, the Project Co-ordinator liaised with the SENCO and an identified school SEA was asked to track pupil performance.

Positive performance records were given to the Project Co-ordinator, either weekly or fortnightly, and the records were typed up in a colourful, pupil-friendly format, and then presented to pupils, with copies given to key staff at weekly progress review meetings. We used explicit positive feedback to ensure that the pupils made the connection between what they were doing right and the benefits for them in terms of being happier, feeling more confident and getting on with other people.

As part of pupil tracking, LABSS SEAs and school SEAs were also asked to identify any concerns about the identified pupils and, where possible, to suggest appropriate strategies for targeting areas of concern.

The Project Co-ordinator met with identified pupils weekly and held weekly meetings with SENCOs, Behaviour Co-ordinators, and sometimes school SEAs. These meetings were used to review progress of pupils, to share pupil achievements and to problem-solve.

More substantial contact occurred in the Secondary Phase with parents or carers, and all were invited to one or two meetings at the secondary school to review pupil progress. This was a useful way of feeding back to parents or carers specific pupil successes, keeping them informed about pupil progress and establishing co-operative working relationships between them and school staff to problem-solve potential areas of difficulty or concern.

At one school, the pupil's problems were thought to be located within his inability to make successful relationships with his peer group, and so the designated LABSS SEA delivered basic social skills sessions for 20 minutes a week.

The Project Co-ordinator offered all schools the opportunity to have INSET on one of the following areas:

- an introduction to behaviour management;
- mentoring/counselling skills; and
- practical strategies to improve the behaviours of pupils in more demanding classes.

Two schools took advantage of this opportunity and the Project Co-ordinator delivered 'An Introduction to Behaviour Management' to support assistants in one school and 'Practical Strategies to Improve the Behaviour of Pupils in More Demanding Classes' to the SEN department in another school.

Towards the end of the Secondary Phase, four of the seven identified pupils were asked by the Project Co-ordinator if they would like to prepare an advice sheet/poster giving information about behaviour changes that they have made in their secondary school. The four pupils showed a willingness to do so and worked either with LABSS SEA or a school SEA to produce this work. The aim of this exercise was to encourage pupils to think about the changes and progress they have made, what they are currently doing that is different, and the benefits of them making better behaviour choices. An example is shown in Figure 8.1.

In the final weeks of the Transition Project, the Project Co-ordinator met with the school's SENCO and/or Behaviour Co-ordinator in order to evaluate LABSS support for identified pupils and to discuss supportive strategies for those pupils after the withdrawal of LABSS support.

Outcomes

The Primary Phase of the Transition Project was effective in providing reassurance to all pupils that they would have some support in their secondary school to enable them to settle in well. It was noticed that all pupils were enthusiastic about the transition and keen to make a fresh start, even though some were experiencing anxiety.

Primary school staff were helpful in giving valuable information about the learning and conduct behaviours of the identified pupils and in suggesting strategies that secondary schools may wish to use in order to manage pupils successfully. The supportive work done with pupils during the primary phase was successful in building a relationship between pupil and Project Co-

My Story

Primary School

- 😟 I would not do maths.
- 😟 I would run out of the room and slam the door!
- 😟 I would interrupt in assemblies – detention after school.
- 😟 I once threw a chair across the room – walked out and slammed the door – detention after school.
- 😟 I would not do as my teacher asked – particularly if I was in a bad mood.
- 😟 I would shout at teachers and then run off and hide.
- 😟 I persuaded my friends to pour water on the classroom floor – we made a terrible mess.
- 😟 I had lots of detentions and letters sent to my mum who was very upset!

"Please don't ruin your life."

Me then!

Unhappy

Secondary School

- 😊 I try to do my maths – I am beginning to enjoy it.
- 😊 I listen to my teachers and try to do as they ask.
- 😊 I put up my hand and I don't shout out.
- 😊 I do not talk in assembly.
- 😊 I do not throw chairs.
- 😊 I have not had any detentions or letters sent home.
- 😊 I am not rude to staff.
- 😊 **I have made a 'fresh' start – You can do this too!**
- 😊 **I am happy at high school because <u>I am trying to change and to do my best.</u>**
- 😊 **YOU TOO CAN CHANGE.**

Good Luck in Year 7

"Be happy at your new school – try to change"

Me now!

Happy

Figure 8.1.

ordinator, though there was not enough time to engage in sufficient project work to cover aspects of making a successful transition to the secondary school. One of the identified pupils had already worked with a LABSS Behaviour Support Teacher, who was already offering support to the school during the last six weeks of the term. She worked with the pupil on how to make a good transition to the secondary school. This pupil clearly benefited from this support. Another pupil already had access to LABSS SEA support via the school system, and this was fortunate because the same SEA worked with him at secondary school.

Secondary school staff proved to be very supportive and liaison with SENCOs was particularly useful in order to establish the support that the school would provide for pupils during the first half of the Autumn Term, and the support that LABSS would give to the pupil and to the school during this time. Thus, a good working partnership was forged between secondary school and LABSS.

Most schools welcomed and appreciated the support from LABSS. Schools found LABSS SEA support to be helpful in the transition period and an effective and invaluable way of modelling approaches to the school.

Pupils and parents/carers found the project to be supportive and three parents/carers of pupils indicated that it was the first time that they had been invited to a school to hear positive news about their child.

With the exception of one pupil, it was felt that pupils made a successful transition to their secondary school and that they were making better behaviour choices. In fact, one SENCO said of a particular pupil, who experienced severe anger problems in primary school, 'It's just so hard to believe he actually used to do all those things.'

In the school where the identified pupil continues to experience severe behaviour difficulties, very little LABSS SEA support had been provided, because of resource limitations. A behaviour programme was designed by the Project Co-ordinator and implemented by the school, but the pupil continued to present problems in the classroom. The situation was made more difficult due to the fact that the pupil's mother could not, or did not want to be contacted by the school.

It was felt that one of the pupils who had made very good progress in his secondary school, and who had a very good relationship with the LABSS SEA, would benefit from further support from the same SEA to ensure continuity of good progress. Consequently, the school decided to buy in three additional hours of LABSS SEA support per week.

The Social Skills sessions delivered by a LABSS SEA to an identified pupil proved to be of benefit and the pupil gave specific examples of what he had learned and how his behaviour had improved at his secondary school.

All pupils who received LABSS SEA support expressed that they valued it, and generally pupils found the weekly progress meetings helpful.

Future plans

This was a very small-scale and therefore inexpensive project. The response from pupils and parents suggest that they felt an increased sense of belonging and involvement and the fact that all pupils remained in school resulted in financial savings for the county. The ASRS team felt that it represented good value for money and have requested a repeat project for July/September 2003.

The Primary Phase of the Transition Project could start earlier, possibly after the half-term break in the summer term. This would then give more time to the Project Co-ordinator to liaise with both pupils and their parents/carers, and time for contact with external agencies already working with the pupil. Unfortunately, not enough time was available for this in the three-week period.

LABSS SEA support could begin in the primary schools after the half-term break in the summer term, on a weekly basis, in order that a positive working relationship can be built up with the pupils before they move to secondary school. This could involve project work with pupils on identified areas of difficulty, for example: peer relationship building; awareness of emotions and of emotions in others; how to manage one's feelings appropriately; awareness of metacognition; anxiety preventative work; and social skills activities.

In order to ensure that pupils are making lasting changes in their behaviour, schools could be offered the opportunity to have Transition Project follow-up support. This needs to be balanced against the need to empower secondary staff rather than encourage dependency on external support. The schools already had funding for supporting these pupils within their budgets – the extra support from LABSS was designed to help the receiving school develop successful strategies. We intend to provide some 'follow-up', partly as closure for the pupils involved and partly as evaluation of changes maintained in the Summer Term 2003. As regular SEA support for schools is crucial to the project's success, increased support of experienced LABSS SEAs could be of benefit and value to both pupils and school staff, and where appropriate, SEAs could deliver behaviour management training with the co-ordinator to school based SEAs who have regular contact with pupils with EBD. It is anticipated that the transition project will be a regular programme within Warwickshire in the future. A framework for the process is included below:

Table 8.1 Framework for the process for the Warwickshire Key Stage 2–3 Transition Project for statemented pupils with EBD

Key Stage 2 Phase

What	Who	How long	Purpose
Initial meeting with primary schools	Support teacher and KS2 SENCO plus school SEN staff	1–2 hours	Information sharing
Joint meeting of professionals from KS2 and KS3	Support teacher and KS2 SENCO plus school SEN staff. Parents invited	1–2 hours	Planning
Meetings with pupil. Observations in primary setting	LABSS support teacher	2–3 hours	Information and data-collection
Social skills/FRIENDS programme	SEA + individual or small group or LABSS support teacher working supporting class teacher in whole class	10 hours	Build resilience against anxiety and problem–solving skills

Key Stage 3 Phase

What	Who	How long	Purpose
In-class support	SEA from LABSS	1–15 hours per week	Observation, monitoring and feedback
Meetings with pupils	LABSS support teacher	2 hours weekly	Information and data-collection, coaching or solution-focused work
Joint meeting of professionals and parents	Support teacher and KS2 SENCO plus school SEN staff. Parents invited	2–3 hours in total	Sharing of information, planning and feedback
Social skills/FRIENDS programme	SEA + individual or small group or LABSS support teacher working supporting class teacher in whole class	10 hours	Build resilience against anxiety and problem-solving skills
INSET	FRom LABSS support teacher on classroom management techniques for school staff	Maximum of 5 hours per school	
Handover and future planning meeting	LABSS support teacher and school EBD co-ordinator	1 hour	Planning for handover and future strategies

9

New technology: services for children out of school

David Teece and Kevin Mulryne

Editors' introduction

David Teece and Kevin Mulryne describe a service for learners unable to attend school that is innovative on a number of levels. First, it harnesses the potential of ICT to change workloads and ways of working to improve social inclusion and curriculum engagement. Secondly, it provides an example of a partnership with a commercial organisation in developing the electronic learning infrastructure for the service. Thirdly, it shows how LEAs can work as part of consortia in developing, delivering and maintaining a service to otherwise vulnerable pupils.

Focus

Educating children who are unable to attend school presents many challenges. Recent changes to UK legislation have placed pressure upon LEAs to provide full curriculum entitlement quickly and effectively. Teacher shortages and the reduction of early retirement opportunities, however, have impacted upon LEA services which have often, in the past, relied upon a supply of such teachers to provide this service. The demands of the National Curriculum, especially at Key Stages 3 and 4, have also brought into question the efficacy of using general subject teachers to provide increased entitlement to the specialised secondary curriculum.

Warwickshire LEA established the IRIS on-line learning system in April 2001 as one possible solution to some of these pressures. It was the result of several years of research and development into alternative approaches to the delivery of the secondary curriculum to children who are absent from school. This chapter outlines the development of this innovative system, from pilot project into an established service that is now the subject of a UK-wide public–private partnership.

Context

It is estimated that there are annually some 100,000 children and young people in the UK who require education outside school because of illness or injury. In addition, there are a significant number of children and young people who experience clinically defined mental health problems. The situations of these children and young people will vary widely but they all run the risk of a reduction in self-confidence and educational achievement (DfES/DoH 2001).

The recently published statutory guidance, *Access to Education for Children and Young People with Medical Needs* (*ibid.*), also requires LEAs to provide education for those children after 15 days absence from school. In addition, this document expects LEAs to move towards an increased curriculum entitlement for all sick children. Given current teacher shortages, it is becoming increasingly necessary to find solutions that are both expedient and cost-effective.

ICT is proving a successful tool for delivering education to children in and out of school, and it offers the double advantage of being generally valued by young people and also being particularly suitable to both synchronous (at the same time e.g. telephone and chat) and asynchronous (not at the same time e.g. e-mail) learning.

Children out of school often become disadvantaged through curriculum discontinuity and social isolation. ICT solutions offer the potential for not only enhancing curriculum provision but also for providing peer group interaction and opportunities for collaborative working.

The IRIS on-line learning system

The system delivers lessons in English, Maths and Science, with other learning opportunities in technology, ICT and PSHE. All children are supported with regular visits.

After initially experimenting with e-mail teaching, we quickly realised the potential of pupils receiving web-based lessons written for them by their tutors. We had already seconded four experienced curriculum specialists (teachers) for a single afternoon a week, who had begun to develop approaches to the construction of 'elegant, interactive' on-line lessons. These posts have been expanded gradually to a position where we have approximately four full-time curriculum specialists. The original teachers were trained to use Macromedia Dreamweaver™ and Fireworks™ to produce the pages after expressing a wish to be in control of the development of the materials. The original concept was that the website administrator, Kevin Mulryne, creator of the website and already experienced in the use of both programs, would add all the interactive and graphical elements after the basic lesson had been written in a simple format. As we could not find an English specialist, this is the system used for the English lessons written by a head of department at a secondary school in Suffolk and sent to us in Word™ format. The need for control expressed by the curriculum specialists, however, led us into costly training in the use of complex, difficult-to-use software. As mentioned below, this issue has now been tackled through the adoption of Macromedia Contribute™, a new, intuitive piece of software for adding content to websites and will be further refined by learneXact™ technology that is being developed by the Nisai-Iris Partnership.

These developments were in response to the state of the educational internet at the time. A great deal of revision material was in existence, as were countless useful educational sites, many of them American, but what was missing were actual lessons and the ability to adapt what was available to the teacher's own style of teaching or, more importantly, the pupils' individual styles of learning. This is a recurring theme in the development of the IRIS system and one that we are only now moving towards solving.

A pilot group of ten pupils were chosen for their high levels of motivation and ICT capability. We had set up a website for the pupils taught by the outside providers but this only consisted of a place to post news and general pupil contacts. It was not until we made the decision to start providing on-line lessons to the pilot group that the concept of an IRIS–supported learning website was born.

The first IRIS site had password-protected entry to pupils' own pages where the work for the week, written by the curriculum specialists, was posted by the administrator. The work was completed by the pupils, usually in Microsoft Word™ and sent back to the curriculum specialist through standard e-mail. As we moved into the highly pressurised arena of providing individual on-line lessons to ten pupils every week in four subjects, we had to scale down our idealistic notions of web page interactivity. We had the technology to develop drag and drop, text entry, cloze procedure or quiz-type activities, but there simply was not the time to do so. Our pages still aspired to the goal of 'elegant, interactive' learning experiences for the pupils, but this was now achieved through house-style rules governing the text and graphics we presented and through links to the pre-existing interactive websites we had identified.

The pilot groups of ten pupils were in rural and urban parts of the county. This meant that, although they were all loaned the same laptops, internet connection speeds were very variable. We kept our content as simple as possible so that download times would not become problematic. The children were at home but, even so, long download times would have been frustrating. Similarly, we made sure that web standards were adhered to and that few downloaded plug-ins (additional software) were required to view and use the content.

Feedback from the pilot group was favourable. Comments included a reduction in the sense of isolation of pupils and parents and an increase in quality and quantity of the teaching provided.

As we learned more about on–line working, we developed the website to include rudimentary mail and news systems, message boards and user profiles.

The development of the IRIS system into a full learning management system/Virtual Learning Environment (VLE) has always been our intention. During the first year of operation there were approximately 12 pupils working on the system at any one time, and the use of a full VLE was simply unnecessary. All we wanted to do was to get the work to the children and receive their responses. However, with numbers approaching 35 concurrent users and the potential for this to increase after the inclusion of Pupil Reintegration Unit pupils, we now recognise the need for a fully featured Learning Content Management System (LCMS). The original IRIS system was based on the manual creation of links and content and was heavily dependent on technical staff's time (as is the case with even some of the largest websites such as www.bbc.co.uk). The weekly routine of maintaining and updating the website will soon become more than we can manage and so we will be moving the operation to the LCMS under development by the Nisai-Iris Partnership (see below) called learneXact™. We were hoping to develop our own VLE based on the open source system designed by Learning and Teaching Scotland, known as Pioneer™ but have not had the development time necessary to see this through. This was another important factor that led to the creation of the Nisai-Iris Partnership.

The IRIS system provides asynchronous on-line lessons and has revolutionised the quality and quantity of lessons reaching children away from school with medical conditions in Warwickshire. Subsequently, the introduction of LearnLinc™ synchronous virtual classroom technology provided a further advance in our provision. Our blended solution up until this point had consisted of web lessons once a week, visits perhaps once a fortnight by all curriculum specialists and e-mail/telephone learning support. This already provided our pupils with significantly more quality specialist time than had been available before the IRIS system and learning time (as opposed to one-to-one teacher contact time) had risen dramatically. However, the LearnLinc™ virtual classroom offers us the opportunity to increase the amount of synchronous teacher–pupil interaction as well to introduce collaborative learning – something that had been very difficult to arrange previously. Pupils use their web browser to log into the LearnLinc™ classroom at the same time as their curriculum specialist and peers. The software works well even over the range of dial-up connections pupils have access to in different parts of Warwickshire. All pupils have microphone and headphone sets and use their standard computers. The curriculum specialist controls the 'floor' and can be heard by all the pupils. He can then 'pass the floor' to a pupil and everyone can hear their two-way conversation. Live video streaming is also possible through standard web cams. The content of the lesson is prepared by the curriculum specialist using a range of tools including on-screen whiteboard, PowerBoard™ (which automatically converts standard Microsoft PowerPoint™ files into LearnLinc™), standard websites (including the existing Iris content) accessed by all through shared browsers, quick Questions and Answers and Application Share™. This last item enables the pupils to see a program running on the curriculum specialist's computer, even if they do not have that program installed on their computer. Reverse Application Share™ is also possible where any pupil can share an application that is only installed on their machine. Tools available to the pupils include live text chat, 'virtual hand raises' and the ability to work in breakout groups, organised by the curriculum specialist, to which pupils are assigned to discuss and then feed back.

Warwickshire pupils have assimilated LearnLinc™ skills very quickly with only five minutes' training necessary in most cases. Curriculum specialists have also become very confident with the technology in a short time as well.

The birth of the Nisai-IRIS Partnership will bring with it further improvements to our provision in Warwickshire. The existing Iris content will be developed by professional web designers and programmers, and will also be broken down into small parts. The desire of teachers to use individual elements to build up their own on-line lessons drives a move towards the granularisation of the materials. The concept of granular learning materials is to take a web page which might be composed of several different elements such as text, graphics, video, animation and web links, and to sort it into a set of separated smaller files or 'granules' which can be stored in a content repository. In other words, it is the breaking down of complex learning materials into smaller, less complex, elements. Once all the content is reduced to small granules then the job of re-purposing them into new learning materials is simple. Our approach is to store all our content in granular form in a content repository as part of our LCMS. The learneXact™ software under development by Italian company GiuntiLabs and the partnership will enable teachers to search for completed lessons or individual elements and quickly and easily combine them to create their own versions, differentiated for their pupils. They will also be able to write their own content and have it added to the database. LearneXact™ also has facilities for setting work for pupils asynchronously and is to be integrated with LearnLinc™ to provide instant access to the synchronous virtual classroom. These features along with advanced tracking of pupil progress will take us even further in the next few years.

The Nisai-IRIS partnership

By the beginning of 2002 Warwickshire's IRIS on-line learning system was providing curriculum input for a growing number of sick children. It was gaining wider recognition and interest around the UK as more LEAs became challenged to provide improvements in curriculum delivery for these isolated groups of learners. Owing to expressions of interest from other UK LEAs, it was decided to offer an IRIS Open Day in April 2002. Representatives attended the event from ten UK LEAs and several other organisations. As a result of an invitation to present IRIS at the DfES Invitation Conference, 'Access to Education for Children and Young People with Medical needs', in York, May 2002, there were several direct approaches from LEAs wishing to purchase access into the IRIS system.

As the system developed, a number of issues were identified. However good the curriculum on offer, there was still concern about the lack of social interaction for the pupils, the demands of producing individual weekly lessons, the time spent by teachers travelling between homes and the limitations for teaching without classroom interactivity.

Right from the start of the project it had been anticipated that the use of a Virtual Learning Environment would allow greater opportunities to build in more interactive learning experiences for the children. It was also hoped that such a product would enable the replication of some of the teaching and learning approaches which children can experience in the ordinary classroom. We met with Nisai Education who demonstrated LearnLinc™, their US-designed virtual classroom and we were sufficiently interested to enrol for trials of the product. This association has led not only to the adoption and use of this technology in WCC but also to the creation of a national consortium of LEAs who share the common purpose of improving and enhancing curriculum provision for children and young people out of school through the use of ICT.

Both Nisai Education and ourselves identified enormous potential to develop an innovative programme that connected with government initiatives, delivering a focused educational service to children and educators. A partnership was suggested as one of the more effective mechanisms on which to build a solution. Discussions and negotiations began in late May 2002 to develop a framework agreement in which Warwickshire CC and Nisai Education would work to deliver their joint aims and objectives. The agreement would set the foundation on which the parties would develop and deliver an on-line virtual classroom network and extend and develop the IRIS on-line education system.

The objectives of the agreement were to:

- provide a clear statement of the respective roles of the two organisations;
- ensure clear and open avenues of communication between the parties at all levels;
- agree a long-term, strategic commitment from both organisations and create a formal framework agreement on which the parties could establish a partnership and provide an agreed framework and contractual arrangements which would enable us to:
  - identify and agree shared development, implementation and marketing costs;
  - identify and agree teaching resources used for creating and delivering an effective virtual classroom and related facilities to meet the educational needs of pupils out of school and educators;
  - clarify arrangements for revenue shares, payment and financial management regulations and confidentiality.

Warwickshire County Council's role in the agreement was to:

- provide access to the IRIS on-line learning system and existing curriculum content for the purpose of the project;
- identify and provide new course content and subject matter after consultation with stakeholders through the content committee;
- ensure consistent standards for all course content through agreed quality control mechanisms;
- provide advice on the pedagogic and technical design of new curriculum content, and the appropriateness of content – providing a leading role in the content committee;
- support the marketing and sale of the product by attendance at conferences, exhibitions and presentations;
- advise on the strategic direction of product development after consultation with stakeholders;
- provide financial management standards and practices for the delivery of the agreement;
- provide advice on WCC internal technical infrastructure and best practice in terms of operational standards;

- advise on security requirements and standards;
- advise on internal issues that may impact on the success of the project such as strategic decisions, technical infrastructure and resource availability.

Nisai Education's role was to:

- provide the hub for the programme including office space and hosting site providing members with access to the network;
- provide training at all levels to ensure the successful delivery of the product;
- repurpose content – redesign the aesthetic features and usability of IRIS and continually update, redevelop and manage the content;
- set up a content committee who will be responsible for agreeing the content before going live;
- jointly review the content committee;
- manage the framework agreement ensuring that there is the necessary and adequate resources to deliver the project;
- liaise with and manage other suppliers, partnerships and organisations involved in the project;
- market the partnership to other LEAs, schools and other educational bodies, and provide financial management and audit.

Lessons learned

There are several issues that need careful thought when embarking on this type of project. Obviously, any products trialled must be suitable for the intended purpose – Learnlinc™ has proved to be ideal, being easy to use and providing a good and useful range of tools. More importantly, there must be good and responsive UK-based support for the product and for the staff who will use it. Nisai Education has delivered in both senses, providing a very reliable virtual classroom, extensive training and excellent back-up. Furthermore, we discovered early on that we shared a common vision for the future of e-learning and we have worked extensively with Nisai Education to develop a possible solution which will be available to local education authorities and other users across the UK in the very near future.

After a preliminary research phase our joint developments have now been formalised into a partnership that is open to any LEA in the UK to join. At the time of writing, the partnership has 13 member LEAs and is about to hold its first conference. Over 40 LEAs have given their commitment to attend with a significant number seriously considering membership. It is anticipated that membership will also be made available to individual schools and other educational establishments.

Our collaboration with Nisai Education has benefited us significantly. We would not have made such rapid progress on our own. The future learning opportunities for children in Warwickshire will, we are sure, continue to expand and improve through our joint work and many more children around the country might soon be introduced to similar experiences through our Nisai-IRIS Partnership.

10

Local learning groups and clusters: the potential of working in an integrated team with groups of schools

Linda Samson and Maggie Stephenson

Editor's introduction

Having looked at a number of case studies around particular types of need and service/agency working which demonstrate many of the aspects of the well-developed service outlined in our model, Samson and Stephenson tackle the difficult area of collaborative partnerships to promote inclusive practice within the context of school improvement. They set out the issues faced by teams willing to work in an integrated fashion and focus particularly on the need for a form of working that enhances rather than reduces professional roles. Their work is highly pragmatic and concerned with 'joined-up' doing as well as 'joined-up' thinking. The nature of the work, which is cluster-based, involving both schools and services, demonstrates the potential that 'integrated' teams hold for community-based working that can encompass a wide range of additional educational and social needs.

Introduction

This chapter describes our experience over the past two-and-a-half years of working with schools and services to develop collaborative partnerships that promote inclusive practice and strengthen the links between inclusion and the school improvement agendas. It has been a journey of exploration and experimentation where we have had to challenge not only our own practice but also that of colleagues. We have discovered factors that either help or hinder partnerships working well together and some things that seem to work for some and not for others. What follows is the development of ideas and practice based primarily on our practical experiences. Colleagues and the many people we work with in schools and in the wider sphere of our work as LEA officers have influenced our thinking and development. Our grateful thanks go to them all for their generosity and support.

Background

The Salamanca Statement (UNESCO 1994) called on governments to adopt the principle of inclusive education for all. Since then, there has been a plethora of government policy, legislation and guidance promoting inclusion and a range of initiatives and regeneration strategies aimed at improving community and economic wellbeing, raising educational attainment and developing skills and lifelong learning. While the separate effects of poverty, social exclusion, poor health, crime, family breakdown and poor educational attainment are well known, there is now strong evidence to suggest that these issues are inextricably linked.

Tackling these interlinked issues is obviously a complex and complicated challenge. The expectation from government is that statutory agencies should develop ways of working together and, with other organisations and community groups, provide an integrated response to the needs of children and their families and provision for groups of children and young people with specific needs who may be vulnerable to exclusion. In other words, enabling 'joined-up doing' underpinned by 'joined-up thinking'. This has resulted in a range of multiagency strategies and initiatives targeting areas such as early years provision, adult and family learning, truancy and teenage pregnancy.

In education, major policy and legislative developments in this area have significantly promoted educational inclusion as part of the broader school improvement agenda. That education should be at the heart of the social inclusion agenda was underlined in the conclusion of the Ofsted and Audit Commission Report (2002): 'the success or otherwise of LEAs is … most likely to be judged by their effectiveness in raising standards and overcoming the effects of socioeconomic disadvantage'. More recently, alongside the requirements on agencies and services to collaborate, the government has actively encouraged neighbourhood schools to work together in order to better meet the needs of all children and young people within the community. This expectation on schools to meet a greater diversity and complexity of need has come at a time of increased delegation of LEA funding to schools, resulting in a need for greater local accountability.

These initiatives are exciting and most welcomed. However, they also pose a number of significant challenges for LEAs, organisations and support agencies, namely:

- how to support schools to work collaboratively and develop an understanding that school improvement and inclusion are inextricably linked;
- how to ensure effective specialist service support to schools within a context of reduced retained services;

- how to work with our community and agency partners to drive forward and shape the broader social inclusion agenda while at the same time striving to achieve the targets set by Ofsted and the DfES for school standards and improvement; and
- how to overcome the potential for conflicting priorities.

The practice of schools and services working together is not new. What is new is the concept of joint responsibility for the education and care of all children and young people within the local community. To achieve this requires a shift away from a culture of interschool competition and the perceived conflict between the standards and inclusion agenda towards an ethos of collaboration. However, collaboration does not just happen. The development of collaborative practice is a complex and evolutionary process that requires skilful facilitation within a developmental framework that incorporates robust mechanisms and structures.

What follows are some examples of how our colleagues and ourselves attempted to address these challenges in Kent, a large and diverse county.

Making it happen – the Kent experience

Through a new policy for special educational needs, 'All Together Better' (Kent CC 2000), Kent LEA developed an extensive programme of action to promote inclusion as an integral part of the broader school improvement agenda with collaborative working at its heart. The main thrusts of the policy were:

- helping all schools and preschool providers to include more children with SEN in their day-to-day teaching, raising achievement for all;
- regrouping resources at a local level;
- cutting red tape and creating a local support team to advise on best practice for a group of schools; and
- giving local communities a greater say in how their resources are best used.

The implementation of this policy was supported by a strategic approach which

- realigned schools, education support services and multiagency forums to match District Council Boundaries (12 in Kent); and
- brought schools together in groups to work more closely with each other and with local support teams.

In addition to these structural changes the LEA appointed a new team of third-tier officers (District Development Officers) to lead the implementation at a local level.

Supporting schools to work collaboratively and develop an understanding that school improvement and inclusion are inextricably linked

It was agreed that the initial focus should be on supporting schools to come together to form Local Learning Groups (LLGs) as a means of working in partnership to meet the needs of all pupils in anticipation of the new SEN Code of Practice and the change in funding arrangements. The expectation at that time was that these new arrangements would promote a change in culture that would assist in the development of improved and more inclusive practice in schools. Since then, with the realisation that collaborative practice enhances schools' capacity to meet the needs of all pupils, and ultimately supports the raising of standards and school improvement, this collaborative agenda has broadened to encompass all aspects of education.

The process

Given that in recent years schools have felt overwhelmed by new initiatives, it was critical that this change in practice be seen as a support to schools in meeting the needs of their pupils. Thus engaging head teachers in discussion about the potential benefits of working together in order to foster a shared philosophy and purpose was seen as an essential first step to establishing LLGs.

The following example (Table 10.1) summarises some important issues that schools identified as the potential benefits.

Table 10.1 Extract from Local Learning Groups Toolkit 2002, Kent County Council

Issue	Potential Benefits
Inclusion	<ul><li>Access to the help and expertise of other schools in providing for pupils with needs outside my school's previous experience</li><li>Plan for future provision of places and a more equitable spread of intake</li><li>Schools can plan together to address provision for disabled access via a local strategy rather than ad hoc selective improvements</li></ul>
Ofsted	<ul><li>Evidence that we are not working in isolation and have identified areas for development</li></ul>
Funding	<ul><li>By pooling funds we can access quality training and call on the expertise of the group</li><li>Group projects using, e.g. Standards Fund, Networked Learning Communities</li><li>There is always someone better at bidding than you are!</li><li>Bids from partnerships are generally more successful</li></ul>
Curriculum, Teaching and Learning	<ul><li>Sharing expertise for curriculum differentiation</li><li>Providing an environment of innovation</li><li>Collaborative projects</li><li>Shared resources</li><li>Joint Training and Development</li></ul>
Fewer support staff	<ul><li>Optimising specialist expertise by identifying common areas of need</li><li>Allocation of service time to the group</li><li>Focus on teacher skills rather than pupil deficit</li></ul>

Having explored the potential benefits of working together schools could then agree the purpose and aims of the LLG. Table 10.2 shows an example of the Terms of Reference.

Table 10.2 Example Terms of Reference

Our partnership will work collaboratively to:

- promote inclusive practice and inclusion;
- maximise learning opportunities for all children in our local community;
- find local solutions to local problems;
- identify and share good practice;
- create opportunities for joint training and development;
- attract funding to develop provision;
- use pooled resources to provide best value in meeting identified need;
- foster a culture of innovation, research and enquiry; and
- monitor and evaluate the effectiveness of the group annually.

Clearly collaboration within a group can happen in many different ways, and not everyone has to be involved in everything. What is important is to ensure good communication systems are built into the structure, e.g. meetings, e–working, newsletters and opportunities for sharing good practice. Taking this on board, LLGs identified common issues (Table 10.3) in order to determine the extent of their collaboration.

Table 10.3 Example of common issues identified by an LLG

Common issues:

- pupil tracking and assessment – tracking of particularly 'vulnerable groups';
- target-setting in literacy and numeracy – whole-school approach and layering of targets;
- ICT and its impact in raising standards across the curriculum;
- teaching and learning styles;
- preschool and Foundation Stage – links with preschool settings;
- transition issues;
- Ofsted – preparation and support, sharing recent experiences, good practice and successful approaches;
- liaison support services and agencies;
- performance management;
- networked learning community bids;
- admissions;
- gifted and talented pupils;
- SATs and agreement trialling between phases;
- behaviour issues; and
- pooled funding for pupils with severe and complex need.

From the list of identified issues each LLG agreed priorities and produced an accompanying development plan (Table 10.4).

Table 10.4 Extract from an LLG development plan

Agreed priority area	Transition between school phases – significant number of pupils unable to 'cope' in next key stage
Target	To improve the transition process for pupils vulnerable to under achievement, disaffection and exclusion
Strategies	• Identify a project group • Conduct an audit of current practice to support transition • Conduct research to identify good practice strategies • Identify pilot groups of vulnerable pupils, implement strategies and track progress over time • Produce practical guidance material for LLG schools
Resources	• Supply cover for project group • LEA services support time • Publication costs
Success criteria	• Publication Guidance Material • Improved transition experience • Improved attainments • Appropriate curriculum for all pupils • Improved liaison between schools on transition

It was acknowledged that LLGs needed to be shaped to suit local need and, given this agenda, groups have tended to be cross-phase and geographically close, thus enabling the development of a local identity and a shared ethos as a learning community.

As with any organisation, most LLGs created a management structure with elected officers such as chair, vice chair, secretary, treasurer, project leader. While in the early days LLG core membership was comprised predominantly of head teachers, over time this broadened to include other stakeholders, for example senior school managers, subject co-ordinators, special educational needs co-ordinators, learning support assistants, support services, agencies and governors. The following example (Figure 10.1) illustrates one such structure.

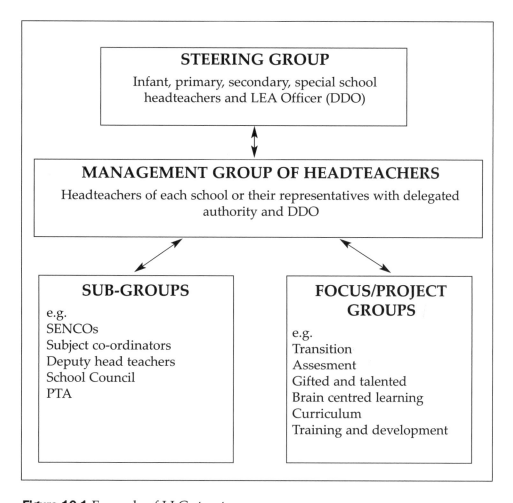

Figure 10.1 Example of LLG structure

Ensuring effective specialist service support to schools within a context of reduced retained services

Where LEA SEN support services have been organised into centrally managed, discreet service units, the difference in emphasis and priority between those services and other statutory agencies and professional groups has cultivated a climate of 'silo working'. Faced with such a range of discreet services, schools seeking support typically resort to multiple referrals in an attempt to separate out each facet of need. Thus, numerous professionals can become involved, each with their own service protocols and specialisms.

However, children's needs cannot be separated into convenient, non-related silos, and clearly, without careful co-ordination, the potential of this approach is, at best, significant duplication of effort, and at worst fragmented, even conflicting advice. Additionally, where services are managed centrally, there are pressures to achieve consistency in service delivery and this can restrict service flexibility to respond to differing local needs, especially where support is allocated on a numbers, rather than needs, basis. These issues have resulted in many tensions, with schools being critical, not particularly about the quality of service, but with the lack of co-ordination and communication between services and agencies, and the lack of consultation regarding local support requirements.

Over the last few years these tensions, coupled with the shift in emphasis from a focus on individual pupil deficit to that of an appropriate curriculum and learning environment to meet the diverse needs of all pupils, have forced schools and services to work together to rethink and redesign ways of working. This has been a particularly important development given increased local accountability and the impact of increased delegation on the capacity of centrally held services.

In Kent this issue was addressed in a number of different ways. First, LLGs were encouraged to conduct and share school resource audits of materials, skills, knowledge and experience. Sharing these resources and identified good practice within and across schools enabled LLGs to release vast amounts of 'hidden' resources to begin to meet the needs of many groups of pupils where previously LEA service support had been sought.

The next stage was to work towards the realignment of LEA support services at a local district level. To facilitate this, a strategic group, The District Pupil Services Strategy Team (DPSST), was established in each of the 12 districts in Kent, comprising local managers and team leaders from SEN support services and co-ordinated by District Development Officers.

The aim of the DPSST was to promote the raising of standards through the development of inclusive practice in the district by:

- enabling services to more effectively meet the needs of local schools and pupils;
- supporting schools to raise their levels of knowledge, skills and expertise to meet a broader range of need;
- improving practice within the team to develop innovative and effective support to schools and pupils; and
- providing support and challenge to schools in removing barriers to full participation and learning.

In order to produce a successful collaborative support model, a developmental framework was used that complemented the development of LLGs.

Initially, many individual service personnel expressed concern that their specialist expertise would be compromised by this way of working.

Interestingly, just as with LLGs, as service colleagues began to experience the benefits of partnership working, creative, innovative collaborative projects developed which enhanced, rather than diluted, their expertise.

As LLG support needs were identified, schools and service staff worked together to produce training and development plans identifying objectives and desired outcomes. In this way, services began to move away from 'silo structures' towards creating opportunities for cross-functional team-working arrangements.

It is important to note that support to individual schools was still available and might require input from a discreet service. However, here too, opportunities for collaborative working were encouraged.

How to work with community and agency partners to drive and shape the broader social inclusion agenda

Through vision and necessity, multiagency working has developed. Across Kent, local partnership working has led to the development of many projects involving personnel from the statutory, voluntary and community services. These aim to develop flexible ways of working collaboratively in order to improve educational achievement, social health and economic opportunities.

In Kent, many of these projects are now linked to groups of schools, thereby promoting the concept of extended schools with 'schools at the heart of the community'.

One such project in an area of high social deprivation has a dedicated integrated team working with six primary schools. Its aim is to develop an interagency best practice model for early intervention and family support services, with a particular focus on children with additional and special educational needs. The team, based on the site of one of the schools includes the following:

- Safe schools officer
- School nurse
- Project manager
- Social workers
- Specialist behaviour teacher
- Behaviour support workers
- Community psychiatric nurse
- Police worker

- Family liaison officers
- Admin support.

The project also receives advice and support from various other professionals, including Healthy Schools, Sure Start, Town Wardens, Kent Council for Addiction, and the Community Paediatrician. The team provides a 52-week service: running after-school clubs, holiday play schemes, drop-in centres and family learning courses, in addition to working with individuals and groups of children within schools.

District planning groups

Taking a wider view, Kent LEA, in partnership with statutory agencies and local partners, reduced the multiplicity of multiagency provision planning meetings, where it was not unusual to find the 'usual suspects' at several meetings discussing the same issues and often the same individual children. This duplication of effort and resources with little overall 'joined-up' thinking or working was rectified in the creation of 12 strategic local forums – the District Children and Young Persons Planning Groups (DCYPPG). These groups, co-chaired by officers from Education, Health and Social Services and the District Council, have wide representation including the District Council, the chairs of each LLG, the Police, voluntary organisations, Sure Start and the Children's Fund. Members also provide links to other fora that, though not ostensibly focused on children's issues, may need to consider their impact on children, for example, the local Domestic Violence Forum.

The clear remit of DCYPPGs is to work collaboratively to provide new, and to reconfigure current, services in response to local need, at the same time exploring opportunities for joint funding and joint delivery. The groups also act as a reference group on children's issues for Local Strategic Partnerships and, in future, will inform the Preventative Strategy.

Establishing clear lines of communication has been essential in order to ensure that each group is represented at all other local groups and to resist the temptation of simply creating a new set of 'silos'.

While the key link in all these developments over the last two years has been the District Development Officer team, LLG head teachers are now increasingly taking a lead role. Thus within a local area there now exist networks and structures that enable collaboration between schools, services and agencies (Figure 10.2).

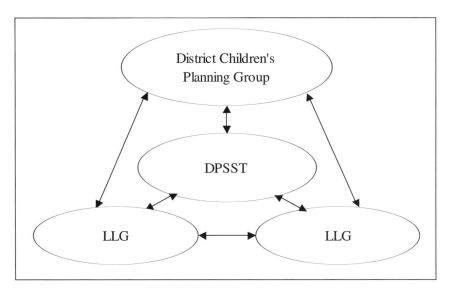

Figure 10.2 District collaborative working structures

What have we learned?

Collaboration takes time!

> The best teams invest a tremendous amount of time and effort exploring, shaping and agreeing upon a purpose that belongs to them both collectively and individually   (Katzenbach and Smith 1993)

Our experience corroborates this statement and the amount of time required should not be underestimated. New teams need time to explore the potential individual and collective benefits and purpose of collaboration. Collaboration should be a means to an end and not an end in itself. In other words, working collectively must be a means of achieving better and more effective outcomes than could have been achieved individually in isolation. Time invested in this way helps foster a sense of group identity and ownership where each partner knows how they can contribute and what they might expect from others.

Guidance not prescription

Early feedback suggested that while forming groups were keen to develop their own identity and did not want 'prescription' from the LEA, most welcomed guidance and information to inform their thinking on matters such as terms of reference and organisational structure and operation. This feedback led to the development of a Local Learning Groups Toolkit (Kent CC 2002).

Working together: does size matter?

Where schools already had experience of working together, the progress from co-operation to collaboration seemed easier and quicker. While it seems obvious that working well together is about building good relationships, we also found group size to be a critical factor. Smaller groups found it easier to arrange meetings with all partners present. They allowed a higher degree of involvement in discussion and debate which, in turn, facilitated the vital development of shared purpose, working intimacy, trust and collective accountability.

Interestingly, as time has gone on, we have found that size does not seem to be such an important factor for groups so long as they have clear structures and lines of communication.

Champions and facilitators

It is well known that change involving the formation of new teams to work in ways that are markedly different from previous practice requires strong leadership, particularly in the initial phases of development. LLGs made a good start where one person acted as the champion for the group. In our experience, a head teacher who had a clear understanding and commitment to the core purpose of the group and the power of collaborative working best fulfilled this role. Champions, however, need support to prevent 'burn-out', and the challenge to all groups is how to share leadership.

We also found that, certainly in the early stages, groups benefited considerably from having someone external to the group to act as facilitator/critical friend and to co-ordinate and make the necessary links between the group, other services and agencies.

A lingua franca and effective communication

In bringing together different interest groups we have found it essential to ensure that we understand each other's professional 'language'. The success of multidisciplinary groups and teams depends upon good communication and the regular dissemination of information. Some groups have found the use of ICT invaluable as a means of keeping in touch between meetings.

Celebrate progress and share success

Those groups where regular updates of progress on activities were provided seemed better able to sustain motivation within the group. In our view, celebrating these small steps significantly helps the group to develop a strong identity and also helps minimise the impact of setbacks.

Creating integrated support teams

The development of an effective integrated team requires careful planning. It is essential at the beginning of the process to establish the purpose and function of the team – ensuring a balance between local needs and the LEA's role of support and challenge. Purpose and function will determine the skills, knowledge and experience required and clear terms of reference should describe the objectives of the team as a whole and the responsibilities of individual team members. It is important to ensure that the specialist expertise of individual members is maintained and extended while developing an integrated response. This will enable individuals to use their specialisms more effectively rather than attempting to cover all aspects of need. However, it is also important to avoid exclusivity, i.e. 'I'm the only person who can do this' and focus rather on 'This is what and how I can contribute to the team'. There should be lead areas for individuals as well as skills and knowledge required by all. We believe that effective teams provide benefits for all stakeholders:

- For children, young people and their families:
    - the knowledge that professionals are sharing information and working together on their behalf;
    - they are consulted and involved;
    - they have a total package of support;
    - they receive consistent messages.
- For schools and LLGs:
    - they have a single reference point for referrals;
    - they receive consistent advice and support;
    - they have access to a wide base of skills, knowledge and expertise;
    - they have a 'voice' – an opportunity to participate and shape rather than simply receive.
- For services and agencies:
    - they have a defined specialist role;

- they have the opportunity to develop other skills;
- they have access to other professionals;
- they have greater capacity for joint problem-solving;
- they have a real team ethos.
- For the LEA:
  - they are able to meet government aspirations for joint working;
  - they are able to deliver more effective support and better outcomes for children, young people and families;
  - they are able to meet requirements of Best Value and accountability.

Does it work?

Since the introduction of the ATB programme in 2001 we have seen the establishment of 47 Local Learning Groups, district multidisciplinary and multiagency teams and a range of integrated team projects involving local community services and voluntary agency partners. While these are all at different stages of development there is a real sense of energy, motivation and commitment across groups of schools and a growing tangible atmosphere of collaborative working. This is in evidence in the sharing of information, resources, funding and development of inclusive practice. In addition many schools, working with services and agencies, have begun to fully embrace collective responsibility in finding innovative ways for local solutions.

While it is too soon to claim that these new ways of working have made a significant impact on school standards, the early indications are that a more joined-up approach does make a real difference.

Examples of the benefits identified so far for particular groups of schools:

- a reduction in exclusions and an increase in attendance rates in schools supported by integrated teams;
- schools are employing and sharing support personnel;
- schools pool funding for joint training and development activities;
- schools agree to common development day closures to facilitate a wide range of CPD;
- specific professional groups, e.g. ICT co-ordinators, arts co-ordinators, within the group of schools meet regularly to share and develop ideas and practice;
- project focus groups are established involving schools, agencies and services, for example on improving the transition experience from Key Stage 2 to Key Stage 3;

- a higher level of collaboration between mainstream and special schools;
- an atmosphere of research and enquiry;
- numerous parent support groups;
- children's participation groups;
- successful joint bids to secure external funding, e.g. Networked Learning Communities, Children's Fund;
- increased willingness to accept responsibility for all children in a locality, e.g. excluded and hard to place children; and
- increased confidence and competence in meeting a more diverse range of needs within mainstream settings.

The future?

As an outcome of a Best Value Review of School Improvement Services in Kent (KCC, 2002), new structures have been developed to build on, and indeed extend, the good practice established through the development of these collaborative working arrangements. Integrated support teams will be managed and deployed by groups of schools. In addition, there will be closer and enhanced working arrangements across agencies and local communities geared towards the development of Children's Consortia with pooled funding and joint commissioning arrangements.

11

Becoming a business unit: a road to Nirvana or disaster?

David Prior

Editors' introduction to the following two chapters

The following two chapters consider funding issues. David Prior 'bites the bullet' of a delegated service and provides an account of how such a service was developed and why it thrived in his LEA. The concept of the school as customer has significant implications for the role and accountability of a service. In contrast, Peter Gray makes use of recent reviews of support services to raise issues of economies of scale at cluster, LEA, regional and national level. He reminds us that 'he who pays the piper calls the tune', and that the suggested role of support services to challenge schools may sit uneasily with a customer service orientation. More so when the criteria used for the evaluation of services may not be measures of increased inclusion or pupil outcomes, but school satisfaction. Gray also considers how bodies of expertise might be protected to maintain services to schools. To some extent, Prior has the answer in the form of professional development bounties for service staff. Unlike non-delegated services, where expertise has to be unlocked by schools trying to qualify for a service, delegated services have to maintain the quality, attractiveness and relevance of their expertise because it is a product that has to be sold. Gray suggests that delegated services are most effective when responsibility for inclusion is also delegated and owned by schools.

Introduction

What is the difference between a disaster and Nirvana? In dictionary terms, a disaster is an occurrence that causes great distress or destruction. The word originates from the sixteenth century and, literally, means a 'malevolent astral influence'. On the other hand, Nirvana is, according to Buddhists, the final release from the cycle of reincarnation attained by extinction of all desires and individual existence culminating in an absolute state of blessedness. So, in effect, both imply an ending of the old state, but a disaster is a destructive event whereas Nirvana, through the elimination of the *status quo*, leads to the attainment of something new and better.

This chapter provides a case study of the process undertaken by Warwickshire LEA in April 2000, in delegating its Learning and Behaviour Support Service to schools. The idea that the outcomes of such a process would be either disastrous or 'the best thing since sliced bread' broadly stereotypes the viewpoints held by a range of special educational needs practitioners when discussing the delegation of central support services to schools. Having been involved first-hand in the Warwickshire process there is no denying that the concept of delegation is a highly emotive one.

Viewpoint 1: the delegation of SEN central services to schools is a bad move

There are those who are philosophically or pragmatically opposed to delegation. In general, they see delegation as a road to disaster and give some of the following reasons:

- The process is likely to be harmful to some of the most vulnerable pupils as schools may see this as an area of their budget in which they can economise.
- Support staff will agree with schools about the nature and solutions to problems that they face rather than retain their professional independence and state what is in the interest of the children. They will do this in order to please those schools who have bought back services and therefore ensure their continued buy back and future job security.
- Increasingly, support will be provided 'in-house' by schools through staff who are not appropriately trained or experienced and who may have a 'one school' perspective.
- Schools will try to poach the best staff from central services and employ them as part of their own staffing establishment.
- In times of budget hardship, schools may choose not to buy back delegated services and this in turn will lead to potential job cuts and redundancies.
- The tenure of employment for staff in a delegated service is uncertain and depends on the annual buy-back by schools. This will encourage staff to leave delegated support services and look for jobs with more secure futures, thereby reducing the potential 'pool' of expertise available to an LEA's family of schools.

Viewpoint 2: the delegation of SEN central services to schools is a positive move

On the other hand, there are those who see delegation as a very positive move and one that will lead to schools being able to plan and cater for the special needs of their pupils in a much more coherent and logical way. Some of the arguments put forward to support delegation include:

- Schools will have a known sum of money which they can use to purchase the best possible advice and support for their pupils with special educational needs.
- Resources will be better targeted than in the past.
- Schools will have more control over the quality of services which they receive and have a greater influence in the way in which central services work.
- Administration and bureaucracy will be reduced.
- Independent services will be more accountable for the support which they provide to schools.
- Staff in independent services will have to be at the cutting edge of developments in their specialisms if they are to add value to schools in which they work and aid the school improvement agenda.

All of these arguments, both for and against delegation, start from the basis of a genuine concern about meeting the needs of the individual pupils in schools and, therefore, none of them should be dismissed out-of-hand. Depending on the circumstances and nature of the delegation process, it is possible for either the disaster or Nirvana scenarios to develop. At the outset, let us be quite clear, the process of delegation of central support services to schools is a high-risk strategy that does have inherent dangers and difficulties as well as a wide range of potential benefits.

Viewpoint 3: the LEA perspective

Why would any LEA want to embark upon the uncertain route of delegation and bring about major changes if central support services have been performing a valuable, and valued, role to pupils and teachers in their authority for countless years? Some possible reasons for wishing to delegate these services are:

- The LEA has to achieve nationally imposed targets for financial delegation, and SEN support is one of the few significant areas of funding that remains centrally retained.

- There is a belief that through the delegation of support services, schools will be provided with a greater choice as to how they meet the needs of individual pupils, and this will aid them in their school improvement agenda.
- There is a need within the LEA to improve the quality of SEN support service, and delegation is seen a way of achieving this objective.
- There is a belief that central services need to be made more accountable for the support they are providing to schools.
- Delegation of support services will lead to a more targeted use of scarce resources.

Restructuring: the SEN Support Service in Warwickshire

Early in 1999, following consultation with schools, Warwickshire LEA decided that it would retain the funding for the majority of its SEN services but carry out a restructuring process. Part of this process would be to delegate SEN Stage 3 (School Action Plus) Learning and Behaviour funding to schools from 1 April 2000 and to run a pilot project during the autumn term of 1999 in the central area of the county.

Restructuring of the SEN Division took place along the following lines. Funding was retained centrally for:

- pupils at SEN Stages 4 and 5, and this was administered through an Assessment, Statementing and Review Service;
- pupils with disabilities, illness and sensory communication difficulties, and this was administered through the Warwickshire DISCS team;
- the county's Pupil Referral Unit;
- the Outdoor Education Team;
- the Educational Psychology Service;
- the Education Social Work Service; and
- some centrally based core staff.

Additionally, an independent business unit, within the umbrella of the LEA, was set up to provide services for those mainstream pupils at SEN Stage 3 (School Action Plus) who had learning and/or behaviour difficulties. This unit was known as Warwickshire LABSS (Learning and Behaviour Support Service).

This restructuring was implemented in September 1999, with financial delegation of LABSS in April 2000. Before that date all existing staff (teachers and support assistants) within the area support teams had to reapply for their jobs but had the opportunity to state within which branch of the new structure they wished to work, e.g. LABSS, DISCS, Outdoor Education or the PRU.

Pre-delegation LABSS was part of the Warwickshire countywide SEN support service with its funding centrally retained and managed through the LEA. Schools referred pupils whom they felt needed additional specialist support. Whether the pupil and the school received the support that they felt they needed inevitably depended on the finite resources in the central pot and it was very difficult to balance the merits of individual cases in widely varying school situations countywide. This meant that the perception of many head teachers was that the quantity and quality of support provided across the county was variable and inconsistent.

Warwickshire LABSS: the two terms leading up to delegation

LABSS came into being on 1 September 1999 and had two terms to organise itself into an effective independent business unit. It inherited 68 specialist staff, a mixture of teachers and special education assistants, and a mixture of EBD (Emotional and Behavioural Difficulties) specialists and LS (Learning Support) specialists.

Staff were spread around the four regions of the county, largely on an historical basis, and not necessarily corresponding with the areas of greatest SEN need. Initially, Warwickshire LABSS was managed by a newly appointed county manager and four area managers. The brief for this leadership group was to establish an effective, efficient and self-financing independent business unit to act as a traded service to schools.

The pilot project in the central area was rushed, and little time was provided for its planning and implementation. Despite the hard work and endeavours of the LABSS staff involved, perhaps it was unsurprising that the outcomes were mixed, with many schools being extremely happy with the service provided but with others noticing little difference from the past. The pilot project provided little opportunity to shape the future planning for whole-county provision and full-scale delegation in April 2000.

The first countywide staff meeting of LABSS in September 1999 saw a group of committed professionals, many of whom were disillusioned and anxious about what the future held and some who were openly sceptical about the chances of success of an independent business unit.

Some of their understandable concerns were:

- If schools don't buy back at a high enough level, will the service cease to be meaningful and will we be out of a job?
- Will a lack of job security encourage our best staff to look for other posts?
- Will schools vire their delegated Stage 3 monies for other purposes?
- Could high overheads make an external service uncompetitive?
- Will it be possible to offer small primary schools an adequate support service?
- If schools are 'buying you in', how do you influence them about good practice when they believe they need something quite different?
- If you offer schools unwelcome advice will they buy you back next year?

This initial meeting was vital in developing the shape of the organisation for the future. Staff were offered reassurances that LABSS had a future, and a shared vision was developed. It was fairly obvious to everyone present that to ensure future success changes would be necessary both in working practices and day-to-day organisation.

Points for action during the pre-delegation period

Consultation took place with head teachers across the county to ascertain what type of service they thought would be best for their schools. Two senior staff from schools, one a primary head teacher and the other a SENCO from a large secondary school, were invited to a LABSS training day and asked to tell staff what they saw as existing good practice and what they would like to see changed. This was a stimulating and enlightening enterprise for all concerned and promoted a good deal of debate between staff within the service. It became evident that despite their expressed anxieties virtually everyone was committed to making the new venture work and was keen to provide a really first-class service to the pupils and schools of Warwickshire.

As a result it was decided that there was a need to:

- review working practices, especially as there was a perception held by some heads that service staff spent half of their days travelling around in cars or working from their bases, rather than in schools;
- reduce bureaucracy and paperwork through the greater use of ICT;
- make it easier for schools to have pupils with difficulties identified and a planned programme of intervention carried out without the need for a referral system;

- review the adequacy and location of staffing across the county so that it better met the needs of schools and pupils;
- improve resources and training opportunities through a planned programme of staff development, so that LABSS staff were kept at the forefront of new developments in their specialist areas; and
- communicate better with staff in schools, providing regular feedback on programmes and interventions and also obtaining their opinions on the quality of support being provided by LABSS and the progress being made by pupils.

Action taken

As a result of consultation and discussion with staff, and through the use of working parties and focus groups, the following action was taken:

- job descriptions were reviewed and revised for all staff including members of the leadership team;
- the annual 1,265 hours time budget was reviewed and expectations put into place regarding the contact time that staff would spend in schools;
- arrangements for travel and the time spent in travelling between schools each day was reviewed and attempts made to reduce this to a minimum;
- the process of recording information and reporting to schools was reviewed and common formats were adopted across the whole county;
- the distribution of staff across the county was reviewed and modifications made to address the areas of highest need;
- laptops were obtained for all teachers, and subsequently support assistants;
- a professional development co-ordinator was appointed and a budget created which gave staff an annual 'bounty' to spend on their personal training needs and other professional development;
- a service level undertaking was drawn up; and
- it was decided to carry out an annual satisfaction survey of 20 per cent of the schools which subscribed to LABSS, thereby obtaining detailed written feedback from all customers over a five-year period. The reason to survey only 20 per cent of subscribers each year was part of the LEA's drive to reduce bureaucracy for head teachers.

Delegating the funding in Warwickshire

The £2.18m SEN Stage 3 funding was delegated on the following basis:

- a £2,000 base allocation was given to each primary school;
- the remainder was divided between schools on a 2:1 ratio in favour of primary schools – this sum was based upon each individual school's Free School Meals uptake and its SEN audit band.

Methodology for providing a service to schools

After discussion and debate, including consultation with head teachers and senior LEA officers, it was decided to offer schools the opportunity to buy an annual subscription to LABSS which would be based on half-day blocks of time. Small schools with low levels of delegated Stage 3 funding, particularly rural primaries, were encouraged to group together and share a member of LABSS staff to allow the service to be more responsive to their needs. If schools chose not to buy in on a subscription basis, they would be able to buy the services of LABSS staff, but at an increased hourly rate. Schools could buy into both EBD and LS support or into either one separately. Different rates of charge were calculated for teachers and special needs assistants. These calculations were based upon the salaries and overhead costs that the service would face in order to break even. As all of the Stage 3 funding had been delegated to schools, LABSS became responsible for earning not only the salaries of its staff, but also the overheads related to:

- premises (including maintenance, heating and lighting);
- clerical and administrative support;
- travel expenses;
- management costs;
- staff development expenses;
- stationery and other resources including ICT equipment; and
- a contribution to the overall running costs of the local authority.

When these calculations had been completed and the rates were revealed to senior LEA officers there was some concern that, although realistic, they might be set at too high a level to attract back sufficient business for LABSS to be successful. It was therefore agreed that slightly lower subscription rates would be set and that the LEA would underwrite any budget deficits (up to an agreed figure) during the first three years of trading. This was an important decision as it allowed restructuring of the service to take place in light of the response from schools, without the need for redundancy of any staff. It also allowed time to develop a strategy whereby the service could explore alternative funding streams to maintain a relatively low level of subscription charges to Warwickshire schools, and at the same time expand as a business. It is interesting to note that from year one the allowed budget deficit of LABSS fell well within the amount agreed with the LEA and that by year three it had substantially reduced so that the service was virtually breaking even in its trading position.

Year one subscriptions

Details of subscription charges and a service level undertaking were sent to schools at the end of the autumn term 1999. Although the closing date for receiving subscription applications was set at the end of February 2000 the service began receiving requests before Christmas from eager head teachers. One of the reasons for these early responses was that schools were able to indicate on the application form which member of staff they would prefer to have working in their school – staff would be allocated on a first come, first served basis. On the other hand, schools who were suffering budget difficulties waited until the deadline before they responded and this made planning for the new business more difficult than anticipated. It also meant that some of these schools were unable to have their preferred member of staff and, in some cases, area managers needed great diplomatic skills to persuade them to take alternative staff. In addition to the subscriptions received from schools, several of the LEA's other divisions bought small annual subscriptions or commissioned work.

In year one, 96 per cent of Warwickshire primary schools and 70 per cent of its secondary schools took out a subscription. Although the percentage of secondary schools taking out subscriptions might appear disappointingly low, it should be remembered that Warwickshire still retains a grammar school system in two areas of the county and this accounts for some 17 per cent of the county's secondary schools. Additionally, many of those schools who didn't take out an annual subscription bought in services at various times throughout the year. The degree of subscriptions received from schools was very pleasing and exceeded expectations, although, on reflection perhaps, this wasn't too surprising, as in year one schools had had little time to make alternative arrangements.

Evaluating the process

The LABSS annual satisfaction survey gives some important feedback on the relative success of the delegation process that has been carried out in Warwickshire. Other useful measures are the degree of buyback that the service has received over the period and also the job satisfaction enjoyed by LABSS staff.

Annual satisfaction surveys covering the first three years

Schools were asked to rate their degree of satisfaction for the specific services which they received from LABSS on a simple four–point scale: excellent, good, satisfactory, unsatisfactory. The combined results are shown below.

	Excellent + Good			Satisfactory			Unsatisfactory		
	2000–1	2001–2	2002–3	2000–1	2001–2	2002–3	2000–1	2001–2	2002–3
EBD Teachers	67%	77%	88%	20%	18%	12%	10%	5%	0%
EBD SEAs	89%	83%	80%	11%	17%	20%	0%	0%	0%
LS Teachers	85%	88%	100%	15%	12%	0%	0%	0%	0%
LS SEAs	92%	100%	91%	8%	0%	9%	0%	0%	0%

When the results from individual schools were studied it was possible to identify particular strengths and areas for improvement within the service. These simple ratings, together with more detailed comments supplied by head teachers, were invaluable in helping LABSS to develop and improve its overall level of service to pupils and schools in Warwickshire. When the results from the different disciplines are combined, the following encouraging picture of progress made by the service can be seen:

	2000–1	2001–2	2002–3
Excellent service	35%	58%	56%
Good service	41%	32%	40%
Satisfactory service	24%	10%	2%
Unsatisfactory service	0%	0%	0%

Level of subscription uptake

The number of individual schools subscribing to LABSS has increased year after year. A much larger majority of secondary schools (including some of the grammar schools) now have an annual subscription with the service. Some Independent schools within the county have bought subscriptions or commissioned projects. Comparative subscription income from schools has risen over the three years from £1.1 million to £1.42 million. Subscription income from other sources has risen from £50,000 to £120,000 over the same period. Each of these indicators is moving in the right direction and indicates a growing confidence that consumers have with the quality of the services being provided.

LABSS staff satisfaction

LABSS recently achieved the Investor in People Award. As part of the IiP process of assessment, staff morale was reported as being higher than at any other time. To quote from the report, 'staff are well motivated, feel valued and appreciated'.

Some of the successes of delegation

Schools say:

- 'we have received a much improved level of service from LABSS which is now impacting very positively on parents, staff and, most importantly, children.'
- 'staff from LABSS are hard-working and dedicated and probably give the school far more time than we pay for.'
- 'we are able to plan in a more meaningful way with a greater sense of ownership.'

Additionally,

- relationships have improved between LABSS staff and their schools;
- the morale of the staff within LABSS is at an all time high;
- evidence from pupil progress and comments from schools indicate that an improved quality of service is being offered; and
- the demand for support from LABSS has increased from both inside and outside Warwickshire.

Some of the difficulties of delegation

- coming to terms with being a business and yet working within the constraints of an LEA;
- building new and different relationships with schools;
- ensuring staff have access to professional development opportunities so that they add value in the schools where they work;
- remaining positive throughout the whole process;
- balancing the books.

The future

Although the income from subscriptions has increased each year, the money from this route alone is insufficient to balance the books. Therefore, additional income streams have to be found and a different management structure is needed to run an independent business. In April 2002, LABSS moved away from the traditional educational leadership model towards one which is more business-oriented, with a board of executive directors. The original leadership group of five was reduced to four who each have specific spheres of accountability – Strategic Director, Subscriptions Director, Training and Consultancy Director and National Initiatives Director. The board is also extended for certain meetings to include the attendance of the Professional Development Co-ordinator and a Learning Resources Co-ordinator. The development of training and consultancy opportunities, and taking the lead in national initiatives, is seen as a key element of the service's future growth. Even in their first year of operation these areas have already begun to produce worthwhile results and new income streams to supplement the annual subscriptions.

Summary

Delegation has proved to be both a frightening and an exciting experience with all staff having to move outside their previous 'comfort zones'. It would be fair to say that delegation of Stage 3 funding in Warwickshire has certainly not been a disaster in terms of great distress or the destruction of the service. Although there has been a reduction in staffing there have been no compulsory redundancies and staffing levels are now growing again. Schools report a very high level of satisfaction with the service they receive from LABSS and exciting new developments are motivational for the staff. At the same time neither has delegation achieved Nirvana. LABSS has not yet reached that blessed state, but then again, it didn't have to become extinct to make progress along the delegation road.

Conclusion: Why has delegation been successful in Warwickshire?

- LABSS has been part of a supportive LEA which phased in the move to a zero budget, whereas some LEAs actually believe that delegation is, in itself, a Nirvana and seem to concentrate their efforts in having an active hand in the extinction process.
- There has been a flexibility and open-mindedness of staff to embrace change as an opportunity for continual improvement and professional development.
- Schools in Warwickshire have worked positively with LABSS to help it improve and develop.
- LABSS has a team of staff, led by a strong board of directors, who have been committed to making the new business work for the benefit of schools and their pupils.

12

The impact of funding

Peter Gray

Introduction

Over the last two decades, the extent, organisation and funding of SEN support services in England and Wales has changed dramatically. During the 1980s, in many parts of the country, there was a period of significant growth in services, followed during the 1990s by equally significant reductions in many areas, as local authorities came under increasing pressure to delegate central funding to schools.

In reviewing the nature and extent of support service funding, local authorities have increasingly needed to consider the role that services fulfil and the degree to which this has to be provided centrally. They have also had to decide how far it is desirable or appropriate to maintain services on a sold basis, with schools 'buying back' service inputs with funds delegated to them.

This chapter examines some of the issues concerning support service funding. It attempts to make a link between support service and LEA goals and the way in which funding best supports these. It draws on a major survey of SEN support services in England, which was carried out by the author on behalf of the DfEE and NASEN (National Association for Special Educational Needs) during Spring/Summer Term 2000.

SEN support services and inclusion

The Government's Green Paper *Excellence for All Children* (DfEE 1997) introduced a new emphasis on inclusion for pupils with special educational needs. This recognised that inclusion was 'a process not a fixed state', and that a variety of elements of good practice needed to be developed by schools, LEAs and others in order to ensure that pupils had more meaningful access to education in mainstream settings. In his introduction to the Green Paper, the then Secretary of State for Education, David Blunkett, indicated a desire to gain good value from the large amount of money that LEAs typically spend on SEN:

> This is not about cost-cutting. It is about ensuring that this provision leads to achievement at school, and success in adult life. We want to look at ways of shifting resources from expensive remediation to cost-effective prevention and early intervention; to shift the emphasis from procedures to practical support. (p. 5)

The Green Paper set out an expectation that LEAs, SEN support services and special schools would play an increasing role in helping move inclusion forward and obtaining 'good value for money' from the funding available. It was acknowledged that this was not a brand-new activity and that, in a number of areas of the country, such good practice had already been developing.

Surprisingly, little had been documented about the specific contribution of SEN support services in promoting greater mainstream access or in achieving 'good value' within available funds; and yet some might say that these have been key areas of interest for many services over recent years. However, one cannot assume that the existence of SEN support services *per se* leads to more inclusive outcomes (see Gray 2002a). Both Goodwin (1983) and Dessent (1987), for example, have argued that the greater availability of such services may have *increased* use of special provision rather than decreasing it. There is anecdotal evidence that, like their mainstream school colleagues, SEN support service staff have a range of beliefs and emphases with regard to inclusion, for example, as to how far we need to develop schools that are more inclusive for the majority of pupils with special educational needs before trying to include individuals whose needs may be more long-term and complex.

A key issue for SEN support services, in the context of the Green Paper and the Programmes of Action that have followed, is the degree to which they promote inclusion. In this respect, it is of particular interest to look at how support services and others see their contribution and the ways in which they attempt to influence schools and parents (some of whom may be less confident that inclusion is the most appropriate direction to follow).

Fair funding

In 1999, the new Labour Government issued proposals to alter the funding arrangements for schools that had existed since the introduction of Local Management of Schools in the 1988 Education Act. One of the aims of this legislation was to endorse the previous trend towards maximising the amount spent directly on teaching in schools as opposed to central LEA administration. There was also a desire to ensure a greater degree of equity in funding between LEA- and grant-maintained schools. With regard to SEN support, GM schools received their share of non-mandatory service funding direct through their grant. They were able to use this to purchase services as they required. Access to statemented funding was free (unless this had been delegated to all schools as part of an LEA scheme). The Government laid a duty on LEAs to consult directly and regularly with schools about any central retention, with the expectation that decisions should be based on consensus.

No financial targets were set initially for the percentage of education budgets that should be delegated to schools. However, when the proposals were ratified in February 2000, a target of 80 per cent was indicated for the 2000/1 financial year. This was subsequently increased to 85 per cent for 2001/2 and to 90 per cent for 2002/3.

As a result of these financial requirements, LEAs had, within a fairly short period of time, to consider what they could retain centrally, as well as securing agreement with schools about the basis for any further delegation. Anecdotal reports at the turn of the century were starting to suggest that SEN support services were being significantly affected by these trends.

The impact of delegation on SEN support services: evidence from research

The NFER study

The National Foundation for Educational Research carried out a substantial review of LEA support services for pupils with special educational needs during 1997 (Fletcher-Campbell and Cullen 1999). This consisted of a questionnaire to all LEAs followed by a small number of case study visits. The research provided a detailed 'snapshot' of the state of LEA support services at that time, with a response rate of 68 per cent to the questionnaires.

The study pointed to the wide diversity of support service arrangements across England and Wales, in terms of the extent and type of support available, and in the way it was structured, organised and funded. However, the researchers also pointed to a degree of stability:

> The overriding factor across local authorities at the time of the NFER research was commitment to maintaining support services in some shape or form: services have not withered at the local authority level as was feared that they would before

empirical evidence about the effects of delegation was available. This shows that the benefits of retaining and providing services centrally are acknowledged. It is not just a matter of statutory obligations: the responsibilities for specific pupils with special educational needs (notably those with statements) with which authorities are charged *could* be fulfilled by contractual agreements with schools appropriately resourced to be providers. These central services have been retained for positive reasons at the turn of the century.

(Fletcher-Campbell and Cullen *op. cit*: 140-1)

The NFER research predated both the Government's Fair Funding initiative and its Green Paper (*Excellence for All Children*) which highlighted the need for further progress towards inclusion of pupils in mainstream schools and may have underestimated the subsequent impact of delegation on support services organisation and structure. It also predated the range of Government initiatives on social inclusion, which progressively transferred national project funding away from central service provision to more school-based/managed support systems (Learning Support Units etc.).

The DfEE/NASEN research

A more recent study was carried out by the author (Gray 2001) on behalf of the DfEE and NASEN. This followed a similar methodological approach to that adopted by the NFER study (a questionnaire to all local authorities in England, with more detailed exploration of issues through three contrasting LEA case studies that had a similar response rate to the NFER study).

The questionnaire consisted of three main sections, seeking information on the following:

(i) the current structure, staffing, funding, role and organisation of the full range of each LEA's SEN support services;

(ii) changes and developments relating to four broad types of support; Learning, Behaviour, Low Incidence Needs and Educational Psychology. (Respondents were asked to comment retrospectively on changes in staffing, funding arrangements, organisation and management, together with any use of alternative providers such as special schools and the voluntary sector. They were also asked to forecast changes planned for the 2000/1 financial year and longer term. Views were also gained about key national and local influences that had affected change.);

(iii) approaches taken to service evaluation and how these were being affected by support service changes.

In addition, respondents were asked about their arrangements for monitoring delegated support service funds.

The case study interviews were semi-structured, with a focus on four areas of interest. These were: support service and practitioner *roles*; the contribution they were making to developing *inclusion*; the way in which their work was *evaluated* (both formally and informally); and their experience of the effects of *delegation* of service funds. Inevitably, time was also spent tracing the developmental history of SEN support services in each particular LEA context. A significant amount of data was collected, transcribed and summarised.

Questionnaire responses revealed considerable diversity in SEN support service provision across different LEAs (echoing the findings of the earlier NFER survey). However, in contrast to that survey, there was evidence of significantly greater change, particularly with regard to the nature and funding of services for pupils with 'high incidence needs' (general learning and behavioural difficulties).

There was evidence of increased co-ordination of services, with moves towards more unified structures. This did not imply the development of more generic roles and functions for support staff. In fact, the trend appeared to be towards creating and maintaining more specialist posts, partly linked to 'low incidence' needs and partly to areas that are politically contentious. This was to some extent due to the criteria used by LEAs to decide which elements of service funding were delegated to schools. More generic functions tended to be seen as being funded more viably and appropriately at the level of the individual mainstream school.

The trend towards greater delegation was most significant in the area of provision for pupils with learning and behavioural difficulties. Approximately 5 per cent of the responding LEAs reported that they no longer retained a service for pupils with general or specific learning difficulties and another 20 per cent only maintained a service for pupils of primary age. There was evidence that increased delegation of behaviour support was partly linked to changes in the nature of government funding for social inclusion projects.

Over 40 per cent of the responding LEAs had continued to manage direct provision for pupils with Statements within their central support staffing. However, over half of these were looking to delegate funding for statemented pupils in 2000/1.

A sold element was relatively common for SEN Support Services, with even 'low incidence' services and Educational Psychology teams generating income, usually for post-16 or INSET/project involvements. However, delegation of service funds was not always accompanied by a buyback option, and schools in a number of LEAs were being encouraged to make their own internal arrangements rather than purchase external services.

Increased use was being made of alternative sources of funding and provision. Most of the LEAs responding were using project funds, typically for initiatives relating to pupil behaviour. LEAs were also using alternative support providers, particularly special schools (25 per cent of responding LEAs) and the voluntary sector (usually for KS4 behaviour provision).

The decision to delegate or retain support services centrally appeared to be based on financial factors, particularly the Government's requirement for most education funding to be passed directly to schools. However, in a small number of LEAs, delegation was also consistent with a strong strategic direction towards greater mainstream school responsibility.

In evaluating the contribution and effectiveness of SEN Support Services, LEAs were predominantly relying on 'activity monitoring' and customer feedback (usually schools). Typically, services were being left to develop their own approaches to evaluation, in the context of broader LEA expectations. It was uncommon for services to be explicitly evaluated against inclusive goals or measured against pupil outcomes. A number of respondents commented that this was difficult to achieve in a context where support services did not have direct control (and where they increasingly worked in a more advisory role). However, more detailed examination of the criteria used for judging support service effectiveness revealed the potential for a significant mismatch between services and schools over the degree of emphasis placed on promoting inclusion and managing demand for additional resources. Support services were seen by about half the LEAs to rate these functions significantly higher than schools.

A number of LEAs were clearly aware of this tension and were seeking to arrive at a common framework of expectations through their ongoing communication with schools. However, the difference in emphasis suggested that LEAs might need to develop more sophisticated systems for evaluation of service effectiveness other than exclusive reliance on feedback from schools.

With regard to monitoring delegated SEN funds, only a third of LEAs were able to describe systems already in place for carrying out this function. A significant number (20%) were developing systems following a decision to increase support service delegation. Some respondents commented that they were unsure whether routine monitoring was now regarded as a legitimate LEA role.

The three case studies shed further light on a number of the issues raised. The key findings from these are listed below:

1. Both mainstream schools and LEAs tended to agree that an external input was needed to 'kickstart' the development of greater inclusion;

2. In their view, an external input was more likely to be needed where schools are less inclined to 'own' responsibility (e.g. where there are issues of challenging behaviour);

3. Where schools already owned responsibility for inclusion, support service delegation (with or without 'buyback') was seen as a logical development. However, issues remained about how far schools purchasing high levels of external service for the general range of SEN could be regarded as genuinely inclusive;

4. Where inclusion was not already owned/established, delegation in itself did not achieve this outcome;

5. Where support services were retained, there was an increasing need for provision to be coherent, clearly focused and of high quality, to ensure that services had an additive impact;

6. With a finite number of skilled staff available, there was some tension between maximising the quality of schools' own provision for SEN and retaining a skilled/high-quality central support service;

7. LEAs were having to manage financial demands to delegate funding to schools. However, there was a strong need for SEN delegation to be *strategically managed* to ensure proper transfer of responsibility alongside funding. Where this was happening best, it was strongly linked to the LEA's broader strategy for increasing inclusion;

8. Some LEAs were having to 'beef up' expectations of what schools 'normally provide'. This was often from a position of insufficient initial clarity and officers were having to find strategies/entry points to 'recapture ground'.

The research concluded that a number of elements needed to be in place to ensure that delegation of SEN support was compatible with meeting pupils' needs and achieving greater inclusion. It was suggested that funding, responsibility and inclusion were inextricably linked and that financial delegation in the areas of SEN was best considered, like inclusion, as a process not a state. In this context, there were a number of legitimate barriers to delegation that need to be planned for and overcome. It was suggested that a number of steps needed to be taken by schools, support services and local and central government to ensure that the different strands of current policy were compatible.

Finally, it was argued that central support needed to be maintained for certain areas of activity. However, there needed to be greater clarity at local level about the nature of these functions and how they are best evaluated.

Support service funding at the beginning of the twenty-first century

The early part of the century has seen continuing changes for many support services, in terms of structure, organisation and funding. Their role in supporting inclusion and working preventatively with schools continues to be recognised in Government guidance documents. However, there is less clarity about suitable funding arrangements. Recent changes to the ways in which LEAs and schools are funded (through 'blocks' linked to specified responsibilities) have given further encouragement to delegation with an expectation that schools will have a greater capacity to fund provision for SEN themselves. On the other hand, the Government's endorsement of a broader mainstream support role for special schools (DfES 2003a) implies that there is still an expectation that a range of services will be provided externally.

It is difficult to predict how things may develop over the next few years. It seems unlikely that we will return to the large-scale central services seen in some LEAs in the past. It seems probable, as mainstream schools acquire a greater share of funds for SEN (and become more aware of their ability to make more flexible 'in-house' provision), that purchasing levels for some of the more successful 'trading' services will start to wane. This could lead to smaller, and potentially more coherent, central teams, with a closer link to LEAs' overall strategies for inclusion and school improvement, and a different balance between challenge, advisory and support functions. However, much will depend on the vision and coherence of individual local authorities. Where strategies for SEN and inclusion are underdeveloped, then support teams can become residual or competitive, with the maintenance of specialisms merely adding to existing interprofessional rivalries.

However, there are other options. In its efforts at public service reform, the Labour Government has experimented with different levels of locality organisation, with new superordinate regional structures, free-standing local partnerships and trusts and greater encouragement to private and voluntary sector providers. Any of these could offer a blueprint for the way in which support services are organised and funded in the future.

We are also beginning to see the development of more co-operative models, with schools encouraged to work more closely together to share expertise and manage provision (see initiatives in Nottinghamshire, Chapter 13, and Kent, Chapter 10). The Government has supported this approach by its recent introduction of less restrictive arrangements for the use of delegated funds. Managing support service time at cluster level goes some way towards ensuring economies of scale and allowing more flexible targeting of support for particular individual pupil or school needs.

Key issues

Both research and informal experience suggest that recent decisions in some LEAs about the funding of support services have been 'finance-led' (i.e. influenced by the need to meet Government delegation targets) and dominated by personnel considerations (see also NASEN 1999). In deciding the best approach to funding support services for the future, LEAs need to consider some key strategic issues. The first of these relates to the best way to influence more inclusive practice in schools. If support services are expected to challenge schools to improve in this area, then they need to be funded accordingly, without relying on schools for the bulk of their income. On the other hand, those who believe that developments in inclusion can be more 'school-led' (with head teachers also being realistic about the finite nature of SEN resourcing) may see less need for a centrally funded capacity.

LEAs also will have to consider how to respond to needs that are unevenly (and unpredictably) spread across schools. These are likely to relate to pupils with more complex needs and those requiring specialist inputs that may not be required by individual schools on an ongoing basis (e.g. braille users). LEAs will need to think carefully about how they can best retain (and develop) more specialist expertise, so that their services can continue to 'add value' to the increasing knowledge and skill of school-based practitioners.

Finally, both Government and LEAs need to give more coherent thought to the challenges presented by young people with difficult and challenging behaviour. Whatever the quality of internal school systems, there will always be occasions on which mainstream schools and teachers require flexible support and advice. Behaviour support needs to be provided on a more stable and secure footing, with proper attention given to promoting effective models of practice and better opportunities for staff training and development. Real 'value' cannot be added when funding is short-term and the nature and quality of service provided is so unpredictable.

13

Best value: evaluating support service effectiveness

Rob Skelton

Editors' introduction

Rob Skelton considers how the principles of Best Value Review can be applied to evaluate and shape the development of support services. Following on from Gray's work he outlines additional criteria and themes that can enable a service to continually monitor its core functions and their effectiveness, making use of a range of performance indicators from stakeholder views and experience as well as performance outcomes relating to inclusion. In order to be proactive in response to the challenge of this process, he also considers the implications for professional development of all staff in the service.

Introduction

Best Value as a process has focused the minds of people working in support services on the nature and purpose of the services we deliver to schools, children and their families. It is as concerned with why services exist at all as much as how effective they are. The mixture of an in-depth examination of the performance of services together with the use of analyses more common in a business environment has challenged those services significantly.

Local authorities are required by the Local Government Act of 1999 to make arrangements to secure continuous improvement in the way that they carry out their functions. In doing so they are guided by measures of economy, efficiency and effectiveness or 'value for money'. A key principle of the process is that this desire for change must come from within organisations rather than be imposed. This is a difficult notion for services that have experienced an era of constant change, new initiatives and challenges to establish ways of working. It is this challenge to the ways that things have always been done that forms a significant part of what Best Value is about; in particular, questioning whether existing services are the most efficient and effective means of meeting the needs of users and community objectives. The process assumes a high level of involvement from providers of services and users of services to gain the broadest insight and consensus on the key issues and key priorities for development.

Acknowledging that there will be priorities for development arising from a Best Value Review underlines another key principle of the process – that the whole process must be worth the effort and focused on outcomes, rather than mere compliance with the methodology.

Challenge, consult, compare and compete

The four key elements identified in the Best Value process are Challenge, Comparison, Consultation and Competition, the so-called 4Cs. Service managers will apply these same criteria to their own team and service through the business planning process. The connection between methods for self-review and service outcomes is discussed later in this paper. Each of the four elements is usually broken down in a series of questions which support the review process.

Challenge

Historically, specialist support services are unlikely to have considered the rationale for their existence. The fact that some children in society are deaf or visually impaired or experience behavioural difficulties is evidence in itself that there are needs to be met. So the question of why the service is provided is perhaps the most challenging initially. This leads to the question of for whom is the service provided and what evidence is there that these service users actually benefit in any way from it. It could be that if the service was not provided there would only be a marginal impact on users, but a potentially significant impact on providers.

One would expect users to benefit in some way but it may be that only some of the service inputs are effective in making any difference. This is useful knowledge for any team or service and can help target support where it is needed most and where it can effect most change. However, it could be that the inputs would be more effective if they were delivered in a different way or even by a different team, service or organisation. This improved self-knowledge can lead not only to improved targeting of resources but also to productive partnerships with other agencies who share an interest in that field of work. Ideally, one would see a greater autonomy in user groups such as schools, children and their families in determining their own needs within a context of greater social inclusion for disadvantaged and vulnerable young people and their families. The diversity of needs means that services have to be driven by an inclusion policy that can meet needs and yet protects the needs of the most vulnerable as a priority.

Compare

Comparing one's own practice with that of others has been, and remains, a significant challenge for support services. In order to undertake this task with any degree of credibility, services have to have a clear understanding of what it is they do and to be able to describe that in a meaningful way. The second requirement is that services know what services in other LEAs do, and a third requirement, arguably, is that, in order to make realistic comparisons, services should be measuring the same outputs. All three 'requirements' are problematic.

The 'Business Planning', 'Best Value' and 'Investors in People' review processes should enable services to determine a vision for the service and aims and objectives. The degree to which these are shared and understood by everyone in the service is a fair indication of their involvement in the process, but not necessarily the degree of their support for the aims and objectives.

Support services can have very different structures in different LEAs. For example, they may include support for behavioural difficulties; sensory support services may be independent of support for learning difficulties generally or may be combined with services for physically disabled students. The work of the regional SEN partnerships has already improved the level of our knowledge of the diversity of provision and the problems of trying to make comparisons across them.

Effective comparisons will rely on services being able to compare their 'inputs' with other services and, from that point, to be able to work on ways of comparing outputs. Service outputs will reflect not only the day-to-day work of the service but also how that work links to LEA strategy for inclusion. As an example, Table 13.1 illustrates the performance indicators for Nottinghamshire Inclusion Support Service against the core functions of the service.

Table 13.1 Nottinghamshire Inclusion Support Service – Core functions vs Performance indicators

(Nottinghamshire Inclusion Support Service Business Plan 2003–4)

Core function	Performance indicator
To add value to the progress of pupils, particularly those with the greatest difficulty in learning	Percentage of pupils supported by the Inclusion Support Service who demonstrate adequate progress as defined by the SEN Code of Practice
To increase the skills and confidence of mainstream staff in meeting the needs of children with complex special educational needs within the context of inclusive practice	Percentage of training provided by the Inclusion Support Service for staff in educational settings judged to be satisfactory or better
To support and enhance whole-school practices to raise achievement, through supporting schools in self-review of their arrangements to provide for the full diversity of need, including those children with the most complex needs and to improve their ability to monitor, measure and record the progress of pupils with the most complex needs	Percentage of schools that have received training in P-Scales (PIVATS): • primary schools • secondary schools Percentage of LEA schools that have an inclusion rate at or above the national average
To provide support and information to the families of children with complex special educational needs	Percentage of families whose children were, when under five, supported by the Inclusion Support Service who continue to be supported at KS1
To support the LEA and schools in maximising the effective use of SEN resources	Percentage of children supported by the Inclusion Support Service preschool who enter mainstream school Percentage of pupils in mainstream provision at KS2 who progress to mainstream school at KS3

It is important that indicators are consistent over time for comparisons to be effective, but they must also, from a Best Value perspective, cover the range of outcome, output and input indicators.

Consult

Arguably, the broader the range of stakeholders consulted, the better informed the review process and the higher the level of confidence in the transparency of the process. Some information will already be available to services and there will certainly be a gut reaction about the degree of stakeholder confidence in the service at the outset that may be confirmed, or not, in the process. Where confidence levels are low it is more important to consult widely.

Tailored consultation methods add to the information already available. These might include staff surveys, Area Reference Groups, and seeking the views of children and parents. Discussing their individual support needs with children can not only be more effective in terms of outcomes but also more efficient in resources. Broader national reviews are also useful in this context for specific user groups (RNID/University of Hertfordshire 2002).

Questionnaires to schools are common across a number of services and LEAs, but their content and scope differ markedly. There are also questions about the validity of such questionnaires given that they tend to be very time-consuming. In one LEA the management team of the Special Needs Teaching Service carries out semi-structured interviews with a sample of schools on an annual basis that provide opportunities for a two-way discussion and clarification of any issues raised.

Compete

For most specialist support services that are centrally retained the concept of competition is as challenging as it gets and can be regarded equally as both an opportunity and a threat. Having said that, many services now trade at the edges in training and consultancy work, but the bottom line here is the issue of whether anybody else in the public, private or voluntary sector could deliver these services in part or whole. One option for services is to seek opportunities to work in partnership with other organisations. My own service works in partnership with an independent provider of services to children on the autistic spectrum and their families in a defined geographical area, sharing both staffing and resources and working closely with health services. Such partnership may not be a cheaper option but may provide a more efficient and/or effective delivery.

Evaluating 'Best Value' practice

Each LEA will have its own guidance for staff on the Best Value process, business planning and performance management. However, this is likely to be general guidance and not specifically related to specialist support services. In 2001, the East Midlands SEN Regional Partnership published guidance on evaluating services. The work was undertaken by a task group from the region and supported by SEN Consultant, Peter Gray (Gray 2002a). The guidance was also informed by national research on SEN support services carried out in 2000/1 on behalf on the DfEE and NASEN (Gray 2001).

Features of a good evaluation system are summarised in the regional guidance document around three headings: Outcomes; Inclusiveness; and Enhancing Effectiveness. In discussing these I will draw upon the four elements of best value described above.

Outcomes

The achievement of the service and its individual staff should be reviewed against an appropriate range of outcomes

Lindsey (2003) concludes, in his critical perspective of inclusive education, that 'there is a need to develop beyond concerns about inputs and settings to a focus on experiences and outcomes'. He argues for a much stronger emphasis on rigorous research as a basis to inform policy and practice. Outcomes can be measured at different levels. For pupils with special educational needs there are, as well as the statutory examinations and tests, IEP targets and P-Level assessments, in the range of tools for measuring progress. The concept of 'adequate progress', as defined by the Code of Practice (DfES 2001a), is problematic in terms of measurable outcomes.

For teachers in mainstream schools positive outcomes of services' interventions are possibly: increased confidence which can have the effect of reducing 'referrals' to services; and improved quality of target-setting in the IEP.

At the level of the school or setting, positive indicators would be a more inclusive environment established in terms of reduced barriers to accessing the curriculum and positive pre-admission programmes.

We would expect to see parent confidence levels improve, especially around transition, as well as evidence of actually working in partnership with parents. In Table 13.1 above, the performance indicator relates specifically to the percentage of children supported by the Inclusion Support Service preschool who enter mainstream school, and the percentage of pupils in mainstream settings at Key Stage 2 who progress to mainstream settings at Key Stage 3. A further indicator ensures continued support for parents at the transition stage.

These outcomes should be embedded in service and individual service members' goals

Most services will now be required to produce a business plan that identifies service objectives and development priorities. These development priorities, or some of them at least, will reflect priorities in the Best Value review action plan that is a response to gaps in service provision. Outcomes should be embedded in the business plan with a review of progress on previous targets and related to planning individual staff development targets through the training and development plan and their individual performance management targets. Linking named people to the achievement of key milestones in the development priorities and a rigorous approach to monitoring the process can further enhance this link to individual members of staff.

Goals should be congruent at LEA, service and individual levels

Business planning standards require LEAs and services to take account of the views of staff about priorities and service contributions. Therefore, on one level the plan should be 'owned' by everyone in the service; they contribute to it, they understand it, they understand their role in meeting targets and development work and they can relate to it as a working document. A service plan, however, cannot stand in isolation. On a second level it must link to other key LEA plans and there will be a strategic line running through them all which is not only implicit in the plan but is illustrated and explained. Staff need to be able to see how their work impacts on the strategic objective of the larger organisation.

The performance management process enables managers, team leaders and staff to make those connections between their personal development priorities and the objectives and development priorities of the service, measured by agreed targets and supported by service quality standards.

Efforts should be made to resolve any areas of incongruence

The services need to resolve any differences in emphasis on key issues between themselves and senior LEA officers. A service may be well-organised and efficient in processing referrals and allocating support according to defined criteria and against a range of quality standards. However, such services have a broader role in supporting schools in progressing inclusion in terms of school improvement. Schools can be skilled by support service staff, and by doing so can actually reduce the thresholds at which schools refer. Moreover, services may want to focus their training function away from the broader awareness-raising to targeted input at the pre- and post-transition stages with the intention of raising confidence levels for all those involved and avoiding potential breakdowns in school placement.

Inclusiveness

Individual staff should be involved in identifying appropriate outcomes and in reviewing progress

Review processes such as 'Best Value' and 'Investors in People' actively seek the views of those staff delivering front-line services. Services can use the business planning process to involve staff in identifying service strengths and weaknesses and in planning objectives and realistic targets.

Much of this can be achieved through existing service structures and task groups. For example, strategic development groups concerned with autism or deafness are in a good position to advise the management team on priorities and progress. If these groups also include other agencies and parents then it gives a greater credibility to the process. For those people who can remember Total Quality Management, the concept of 'quality circles' can be useful in identifying any barriers to progress.

Individual staff members are key to determining whether pupils have made 'adequate progress', particularly by supporting schools in making that judgement and thus modifying IEP targets. Staff will also have a view on the extent to which schools are making effective use of SEN resources in meeting those children's needs.

Meeting children's special educational needs should be a co-operative endeavour

Evaluation methods should support a team approach to achievement, within service, between service and schools and between different, but related, services. In Nottinghamshire's Best Value Review of services for children with special educational needs, one of the key themes raised by schools and parents was collaboration between services in the same LEA.

From a Best Value perspective, services that are effective in isolation may still have a way to go in meeting the needs of service users and in reducing the potential for duplication of resources. It requires positive co-operation and joint working between services, and also clearly defined roles and responsibilities for people in those services. It is then possible to develop a single system which records inputs from the service by activity and time and to put in place a cross-service quality assurance system that seeks comment on the effectiveness of the totality of SEN service provision, from a school, parent, child and LEA perspective. All of this should support the development of ways to streamline the deployment of staff from all SEN services, to achieve better co-ordination, better value for money and improved user focus.

The evaluation approach should be permissive of a range of relevant data

Performance review processes can produce a richness of data. Issues around the complexities of data collection and interpretation are not in the remit of this chapter. However, it is important to note that figures, like language, can be interpreted in many ways. Transition figures that I referred to above, for example, need to be linked to measures of confidence if the impact is to be sustainable longer term and not just a feature of short-to-medium-term service activity around the period of transition.

Seeking the views of children can be a particularly important influence on policy and practice. Brian Lamb, Director of Communications at RNID, noted in 2002 that

> It is instructive that while policy initiatives are typically focused on increasing access to the curriculum, the children told us that social exclusion and friendship with their hearing peers was what was really important to them.
>
> (RNID University of Hertfordshire 2002)

The Nottinghamshire Best Value Review of services for children with SEN noted similarly that support from peers in mainstream schools was a critical factor for them. In the same review, a survey of 1,744 parents of children without special educational needs showed that 66 per cent of them felt that having a child with special educational needs in their child's class was a positive experience for their own child.

Evaluation should involve recognising and documenting a range of achievements and relative, as well as 'absolute' success

Outcome indicators should be directly relevant to the LEA's targets and priorities and they should also be realistic in the sense that they will tell us something important and useful about the work we do. They need to be attributable to the activity undertaken by the service. As stated earlier, defining service contribution to adequate progress can be problematic but a first step in defining that progress has taken place at least. Services need to define outcomes as well as possible using sensible measures that all staff, and indeed stakeholders, can understand. Managers in the service need to be confident that they can actually collate data and track progress.

In tracking progress several points are important. First we need an overall judgement that is supported, hopefully, by data. The nature of the evidence base for such a judgement needs to be clear. In particular, it is useful to know which service activities have been most effective and which have had least impact. Finally, it is as important to know which factors have contributed to or inhibited progress and to include the results of such observations in future planning.

Enhancing effectiveness

Self-review should help ensure that professional development needs at both service and individual level are identified

Service development priorities, particularly those that are picking up on gaps in service provision or on new national initiatives such as the early intervention strategies, will require services to identify training and development needs. Moreover, services need to ensure continuous improvement in the delivery of their core functions, consistent with Best Value, by developing staff skills and competencies, identified through performance management arrangements.

This assumes that staff are informed about what the organisation is trying to achieve through its service objectives and vision, and that they are also informed about how they are contributing to meeting those objectives. There is then a strong, explicit link between the LEA inclusion strategy, service priorities and the identified professional development needs of service staff. Meeting the targets related to service performance indicators is a whole-service responsibility.

The assumption of usefulness

This assumption discourages self-criticism and constructive challenge of existing practice. It is important for services to feel needed and valued but continuous improvement demands both external, as well as internal, insights into development opportunities, strengths and weaknesses. It is useful to question even those things that we do well. For example, when parents of children with special educational needs are asked to complete a questionnaire about their level of satisfaction with the service, responses are invariably good. However, it could be argued that what parents are doing here is maximising their chances of retaining the same level of support in the future. It may also be the case that some 'hard-to-reach' parents are not being consulted at all.

Stakeholder or user groups are a useful way of obtaining that external insight into service effectiveness and indeed an insight into how the service appears to someone who does not work in it and may have no knowledge of education.

Common practice is to now pilot different ways of working or working with different partners. This can be extremely valuable, particularly if it is based on core functions and activity and focused on specific, measurable outcomes.

Self-review should help identify both positive and unacceptable practice

Services should identify relevant quality standards for their activities. These set out the expectations for how the service will work and provide a baseline to work to in order to ensure that customers such as schools, parents and children get a good service. In any large organisation there are some common, given standards, such as those relating to customer care. However, they should not be so numerous as to become meaningless. If they are going to be monitored effectively they need to be clear, understood by staff, realistic and transparent.

Services may adopt nationally agreed standards such as the National Deaf Children's Society Paediatric Audiology Standards, particularly where these are linked to national initiatives such as early intervention strategies.

The standards will be published in the service's business plan and this will set out the success criteria and responsibilities for action and monitoring. Table 13.2 provides an example.

Table 13.2 Success criteria and responsibilities for monitoring service standards

Quality standards	People involved	Success criteria	Actions	Monitoring/evaluation – when and by whom
Families will be consulted on the management planning process	Stakeholder group	Direct views and contribution of families are part of the management planning process	Research and identify effective methods for consultation (e.g. via questionnaires or attendance at meetings etc.) Identify families to consult/involve	Stakeholder group will establish families' involvement in management planning process

In a climate of greater accountability it is preferable for support services themselves to develop self-review methodologies – on the assumption that they understand their role – using the business planning process as an effective tool, in the context of delivering services that people really want.

14

Issues for the future

Mike Blamires and John Moore

Introduction

The case study contributions demonstrate a great deal of innovation and good practice and much that promises a secure role for support services in the future. The direction of that future, however, is less certain. A number of issues have emerged throughout the preceding chapters that will need serious attention if services are to attain the state of development we propose in our model. Some of these issues lie within the purview of the services themselves but others, such as the future mechanisms for funding outlined by Peter Gray, do not. In these instances it will be necessary for services to collectively, either locally, regionally or nationally, exert pressure on local and national government to resolve the tensions that these issues create. In the following we outline a possible agenda for consideration.

Working together

It is clear from the examples outlined in this book that there is already a variety of ways that services and agencies can work together to produce effective support for parents, pupils and schools. There are very few examples, however, of what we would describe as 'fully integrated teams'. Interestingly, this does not correlate as one might expect with the development of a 'project' approach to support. There are many good projects described that use only two or three contributing services. The key is in deciding which services are best placed to work together, for what period of time, to achieve what goal. As Christine Salter demonstrates, quite often what is required is an understanding of why certain groups of pupils are not best served by agencies working in tandem rather than together. The 'disappeared', the emotionally vulnerable and school refusers are good examples as to why an 'interagency', rather than an 'multiagency', approach, to use Gill Henderson's analysis, is likely to be more effective. One of the very reasons for LEAs not knowing where pupils are (the disappeared) is the continuance of a model that separates out behaviour service support from medical needs support and Child and Adolescent Mental Health Services.

To counteract this, it is necessary to have structures available that not only bring the respective services together in one place but also provide decision-making mechanisms that use common data sets. This may be feasible for two or three services working together but the issue of database incompatibility between Health, Social Services and Education is well known, as outlined by Marion Russell, and presents a considerable logistic and confidentiality challenge.

Christine Salter's example of education working with CAMHS is particularly instructive here because it is a project that is based on a clear and common understanding of pupil needs and the roles of the participating agencies. The location of an education psychologist within CAMHS seems to have been critical to its success and is described as 'an important catalyst'. This is not just about co-location but 'implanting expertise'. Although respective roles need to be made clear, learning new skills from others is an essential part of the experience.

The real challenge comes, however, when services are organised to work together on a 'day by day' basis, rather than effect a one-off project. Samson and Stephenson rightly point out that to create an 'integrated support team' requires much time and careful planning. It goes hand-in-hand with the notion of working with a group of schools rather than single institutions. They remind us that it is essential that the expertise of individual members is maintained and extended at the same time as developing an integrated approach. This begs the question of organisation and line management. Many professionals will be reluctant to be managed by personnel outside their own profession and some accommodation needs to be made to balance professional oversight and day-to-day working within a project structure. Nevertheless, many good examples are now emerging as a result of initiatives such as Sure Start and Healthy Schools, as well as established networks such as the Early Years Development Childcare Partnerships.

An inevitable further challenge is posed, therefore, by the multiplicity of initiatives emanating from central government, particularly in areas of high deprivation. There may be numerous funding streams each with their own demands on service and agency time. As a result, many of the same agency and service personnel meet at regular intervals for ostensibly different purposes. For some, this has now reached unmanageable proportions. Either the projects need to be rationalised alongside the funding or professionals need to be brought together into a single forum that can take on board all of these developments through properly prioritised work. This would seem to strengthen the argument for the structures proposed by Samson and Stephenson.

The policy context

Implementing 'integrated service teams' on a group-of-schools basis might proceed more quickly if they were not so dependent upon factors outside of the participating agency and service control. As Peter Gray points out, the most influential of these is funding – not necessarily the amounts but how funding is deployed. There appears to be little argument about the fundamental role of LA support services, for example, in that government initiatives continually stress their importance in supporting inclusion and in working preventatively. Without a clear funding mechanism, however, it is difficult to predict how services will develop, even in the context of project activity within clusters of schools. There are some good examples of shared school funding for buying in service activity and of services 'devolved' to clusters (Kent 2003), but there is some way to go before services can feel confident that mainstream schools will view them as equal partners in advancing the education of all pupils.

Two other areas of national policy that currently impact on service direction are government targets within 'silo' departments and the unresolved role of the special school. To take the first, it is difficult to understand why government departments find it so difficult to speak to each other when this is clearly what they want from those on the ground. In reality, this is also a matter of funding. The Treasury sets spending through its reviews and requires departments to be accountable for this spending. The current means of achieving this is through setting targets. Unfortunately, these targets are not always as consistent with each other as they should be, and the 'silo' effect comes into play whereby the minister responsible cascades these requirements to the point of delivery, as is the case with school league tables. Putting aside the issue of tension and inconsistencies that exist between national education targets and inclusion, which is well documented elsewhere, there are subtler impacts that impinge on working together. The lack of a clear focus on children's services as a priority for Primary Care Trusts (PCTs), for example, can only hinder any interagency activity planned on the ground that involves therapies. Given that autism and behaviour, for example, are two major areas of growth for special education, it will be a challenge for local services to provide support for inclusion without a clear commitment from PCTs.

By the time this book is published, there may well be a clearer role for special schools in providing services. What will be less clear, however, will be the potential impact of the proposed changes on the way special schools work to the Government's agenda of inclusion. The DfES Report of the Special Schools Working Party (2003c) appeared to face two ways; towards the retention of special schools and towards further inclusion.

As a result, the working party failed to engage with some of the more important issues around strategic planning. If the proposals of that paper were accepted, for example, there would inevitably be fewer special school places as greater emphasis is placed on 'outreach' services. There is little in the document that recognises the degree of planning that this would require. Given the key role attributed to support services in furthering inclusion, it will be essential to obtain greater clarity as to the Government's intentions on this and, in particular, how retaining special schools can support this objective.

The nature of planning

All of this makes effective planning difficult to achieve. One of the clear messages from the case studies is that early mistakes take a long time to rectify, and that time spent together exploring potential issues is not time wasted. What is also clear from the case studies, however, is that interagency support service activity can also throw up unplanned outcomes of a positive nature. This is because we do not have a ready-made recipe-book for combining different services and agencies and cannot always predict the result. A shared feature of many of the studies, and in particular those concerned with transition, is the 'catalytic' effect of the project, either on a participating service, pupils, schools or group of schools. The ability to harness unexpected outcomes can be seen as an important indicator of effective service development.

The importance of mainstream infrastructure

As Attfield demonstrates, services cannot be effective unless there is a well-developed infrastructure in mainstream schools that can take advantage of the expertise on offer.

Roaf (2002) makes the distinction between upstream and downstream ways of working, which she derives from a folk tale. 'Downstream' working is a case-by-case reaction, whereas 'upstream' working is seen as a holistic, proactive and preventative way of working. She suggests that a school's SENCO may adopt a 'downstream' approach in taking responsibility for a large caseload of similar needs (as illustrated by Attfield), rather than utilising a range of resources including systems within the school and beyond to create more efficient 'upstream' approaches. The key message is to avoid the bolt-on structures arising from downstream working by ensuring that initiatives can be embedded in the school improvement plan and agenda. As the Audit Commission (2002: 42) suggests:

> The debate now needs to move forward in a number of ways:
>
> - from its current focus of 'picking up the pieces' for individual children, to responding to the diversity of needs in every classroom;
> - from a focus on paperwork, processes and inputs, to how each child is to be helped to progress and the outcomes they achieve...;
> - from treating children with SEN as a peripheral interest in education policymaking, to putting them at the heart of mainstream policy and practice.

This point is reinforced from Scottish experience: 'If schools are to successfully implement a commitment to inclusion, they need to give careful thought to how they will evaluate their success in achieving relevant outcomes for the pupils they serve' (HMI Scotland 2002: 28).

In short, if it does not add value by building the school's capacity for inclusion, don't do it; be prepared to modify your activity to improve the structure of the school. Both schools and service(s) need good intelligence about structure and performance. The Scottish HMI (above) report identified a number of indicators that readers may wish to consult in more depth within the report. These include indicators of successful patterns of attainment, indicators of success in terms of broader achievements and indicators beyond school. These might form a better alternative to evaluating the success of support services through school satisfaction, which Gray has found to be the predominant measure.

McLaughlin (1989) has suggested three Rs in relation to the support of teachers: respect for the teachers and their work; reality (start from where the teacher is); and responsibility (which should remain with the teacher). The chapters by Butt and Cosser and Dixon and Gahir provide examples of this way of working where the 'confidence and competence' (Thomas 1992) of mainstream teachers is sensitively enhanced.

In a systematic review of the literature on inclusion in schools conducted by the Inclusive Education Review Group (2002), a number of themes were noted as being important in developing inclusive practice and increasing participation. These included an inclusive culture with shared values and attitudes among staff that 'accepted and celebrated difference' and held 'a commitment to offering educational opportunities for all', as well as a culture of collaboration among different specialisms leading to 'blended services' in mainstream schools that increased their capacity to respond to difference and participate in joint problem-solving. As stated by Samson and Stephenson, joined-up working is needed as well as joined-up thinking.

Leadership

The movement of services from the 'cupboard' to the community has required strength of leadership on the part of individual service leaders, as is well demonstrated in the case studies and projects. Leadership, however, is not an area that many local authority services or other agencies have afforded sufficient attention. Much of what is promoted, particularly in the statutory agencies, concerns management training. The emphasis is on the production of business plans and Best Value reviews that rightly follow the process of the 'four Cs' as described by Skelton, but which neglect the issue of leadership despite carefully worked standards.

Part of the problem here lies in the distance that still exists between many support services and education advisory services, where the development of support service teachers in particular is often at the 'caboose of the train'. Witness the difficulties experienced by many LEAs over the introduction of threshold progression for support service employees on teachers' pay and conditions. Performance management processes were introduced quickly into a system not generally given to this kind of approach. Similarly, the Teacher Training Agency has produced credible standards for SENCOs and SEN specialisms around the four dimensions of SEN, but similar standards are not available for support teachers.

Attfield identifies 'leadership commitment to high standards for all' as a key feature of an effective environment for inclusion. While this is referenced to schools, it does not make sense for leadership within a school or group of schools to pursue this agenda if there is not an equal leadership commitment from those supporting their efforts. Clearly, this commitment does exist, as is well demonstrated in the case studies, but the development of leadership in this context is nowhere near as strong a focus for services as it is for schools.

Hugh Clench (2003) of the South Central Inclusion Partnership has proposed the development of leadership as an essential part of evaluating support services using the EFQM (European Foundation for Quality Management) excellence model and the new Ofsted framework for the inspection of schools. The EFQM model, in particular, makes use of nine criteria split between enablers and results. A substantial part of the enabling process is made up of front-end leadership with innovation and learning taking place through a feedback cycle from key performance results to inform leadership improvement. This would seem to be a process worthy of further consideration.

Many of the examples of good practice described in this book have depended on strong leadership from within a single service. The development pattern we have outlined in our model, however, increases the demand for leadership qualities the further it moves towards trans-agency and community-based working across groups of schools and early years settings. A question for the future, therefore, is 'How will this leadership be encouraged and developed to match the same level of commitment to that currently demonstrated to schools by the Government through the National College for School Leadership?'

School Improvement

Although not always directly stated, school improvement is a common theme in many of the preceding chapters. The overall reduction of LEA staff in favour of delegation, noted earlier, and also the introduction of relatively small unitary authorities, has, perversely it might seem, encouraged greater integration of local authority advisory and support services, many of whom now share common line management with consequent blurring of role boundaries. What is described in the case studies, and most clearly articulated by Samson and Stephenson however, is that concern for school improvement within support services goes hand-in-hand with significant structural change. The development of services, as outlined in Chapters 1 and 2 for example, would suggest that inclusion as a vision was more readily adopted by services than school improvement, although it is difficult to see how the first could have been achieved without the latter.

The business of support services, as shown in our model, must be first and foremost the achievement of our most vulnerable children and young people. It must also be about progressing this within the context of schools' and early years settings' determination to improve standards for all.

While it is right to make the argument, therefore, that the ownership of community-based inclusion rests with schools and settings, consistent with the general movement towards self-managing schools and effective self-review, the broader context of school improvement also demands a degree of challenge.

This, alongside the increased monitoring and intervention roles prescribed for local authorities by central government, will present a formidable change agenda for services specifically located within education. The discussion on funding related above will also have a significant bearing on how this might develop.

This change will require Best Value reviews to adopt and adapt the literature and practice of value added, which, as Attfield points out, is still in its infancy. Best Value alone is too simple a process to evaluate complex relationships between organisations of the sort outlined by Henderson, Russell, Salter, Samson and Stephenson; neither are there sufficient data available to make a reliable 'comparison' between outcomes of 'similar' services in 'like' authorities. The use of 'residuals' to compare the value added from one key stage to another for matched groups of pupils, with and without special educational needs, for example, is rare. It could reasonably be expected, however, that this 'science' would develop with the refinement and moderation of the QCA P-Scales.

At the crudest level, Best Value is concerned with a cost-effective choice being made across reasonably similar alternatives, and value added about identifying 'additionality' or progress made from agreed starting points as a direct result of intervention, challenge or support. This, of itself, is quite a challenge.

A greater voice for learners and their carers

Roaf (2002) believes that the need for interagency work arises from the threat to the life chances of children who are difficult to place or who tend to fall through the net of available services. (This includes the children considered in the chapters by Russell, Salter, and Teece and Mulryne.) These children are at the end of a continuum of learners whose voice is infrequently listened to despite legislation and increasing exhortation.

It has also been suggested by Roaf *(ibid)* that interagency work for children is difficult because of their vulnerability, subordination, dependence and the fact that they are minors who have distinct communication needs. Russell, in her chapter, emphasises the need for corporate responsibility and advocacy for children in care, and it may be that the lack of this is the real reason why children often fall through the net. Lacey (2001) has noted that for children with complex needs, a professional who takes on the role of a key worker is important for successful teamwork. This is clearly the role implied in the work on transition by Dixon and Gahir, and Butt and Cosser. Alternatively, Skelton and Henderson in their chapters note the move away from individual casework suggested by the first Code of Practice towards a more proactive whole-school orientation of the second Code. The HMI (Scotland) (2002) report on inclusive schooling, based upon inspection data, suggested such an approach needs to be sensitive to the voice of the learner and the carer.

The report noted that 'features of good practice in developing an inclusive ethos included: full participation of individuals and groups with special needs in social as well as curricular activities; and high levels of consultation with pupils and parents on important aspects of school life and on the extent to which the school was meeting its aims'.

Butt and Cosser describe an innovative strategy to provide a voice for children who cannot give voice to their needs and wants themselves. It is also a mechanism that develops the teacher's capacity for inclusion. If this is possible for such challenging learners, then schools and services could benefit from using passports to inclusion for other children to harness both the knowledge of the learner and the resources of the school and community.

Teese and Mulryne's utilisation of ICT has enabled the voice of the learner to be heard more frequently through e-mail and chat. This has also the potential for the establishment of a collective voice through an on-line community. Samson and Stephenson's chapter provides an example of the school becoming a community hub so that local representatives give voice to the concerns of parents and carers, which is also the approach favoured by Roaf. The challenge is to ensure that such representation is truly representative and that views expressed are valued and responded to. With an increase in clusters and consortia of schools, the challenge will be to ensure that vulnerable groups have a voice and that one school or service does not dominate the emerging agenda.

Funding mechanisms

The Government has recently experimented with different levels of funding to support schools as a result of devolved government in some parts of the United Kingdom. For example, 'independent parental advisory groups' have been funded from LEA Standards Fund in England, with the consequent professionalisation of previously voluntary or charity-funded parental advocates, so that poachers have become gamekeepers; whereas in Wales, the same function was funded directly by the Welsh Assembly, so that it is free from LEA influence. A similar argument might be made for regional or national funding of support services in their role of challenging schools to improve. Support services, however, have also to be seen as having something relevant to offer schools and clusters. The move towards delegation of funds to school clusters and fora is an opportunity for services to negotiate their proactive role across phases of education. As the chapters in this book attest, some children are at their most vulnerable at times of transition or when they are not attending school. There is clearly a co-ordination role for support services in gluing the educational experience of vulnerable learners into a coherent progression rather than disparate stops and starts across schools.

Roaf has defined competence as 'the ability to do the right thing at the right time for the right reasons'. In order to ensure that competence is in place there may be a need to revisit the concept of 'subsidiarity', where decision-making and influence are organised in an heterarchical, rather than hierarchical, manner, i.e. one that is both top-down and bottom-up. In their chapters, Skelton and Henderson have both noted the way in which funding mechanisms drive practice. The first Code of Practice had an unintentional perverse incentive to move children up the stages to 'secure' provision, and turned support services into gatekeepers or assessors of adherence to protocols. The unintended outcomes of the second Code and the SENDA have yet to emerge.

One solution may be for agencies to have terms of reference alongside their targets or be encouraged to develop shared targets as part of a memorandum of agreement with potential partners, as suggested in Skelton's chapter. Another may be for schools to set targets for inclusion that are linked to funding which may involve some subcontracting to support services in building enduring capacity for inclusion. Gray and Skelton have hinted at what these targets might be.

Where funding for services is delegated to schools and then used to buy back services from the LEA, there can be, as Prior shows, additional advantages for the school and service in that there are economies of scale that allow a service to invest in staff expertise and have a development plan. This plan can be responsive to schools at different stages of development in relation to inclusion. Also synergies are likely to accrue from the service working across a number of settings, networking and being proactive in relation to emerging national agendas. 'Buyback' arrangements, however, should be contrasted with piecemeal 'bought-in' arrangements that depend on the expertise of a 'sole trader' who may have particular and parochial agendas, as well as an uncertain long-term viability.

The additional challenge for delegated services, beyond viability, is how to ensure that collaboration occurs between and across services, as some schools or clusters may not see this as a core function of support. Indeed, where clusters of schools shape the service they receive to their development requirements, it might be argued that the service exists as an interim measure until the school or cluster develops the skills and knowledge that the service currently exercises. This, however, assumes static knowledge and skills and does not sufficiently recognise that knowledge and skill develop from networking across a large number of schools.

Conclusion

These, then, are the issues that need to be addressed if services, and particularly those associated with the LEA, are to rise more fully to the challenge of supporting mainstream inclusion. In Chapter 2 we have set out the vision for this development, and our contributors have demonstrated what can be achieved when there is a determination to work more broadly with the community. They have also demonstrated that support services can be effective in matters of both social and academic inclusion. Our proposed method shows that well-developed services have unique and important knowledge that schools can benefit from, and be positively challenged by. The future of support services will not be in question if they move from the 'cupboard' into the community, even if, in the process, they are involved in delegation, become smaller or more focused on 'low-incidence' needs. All contributors to this book share the view that support services play a vital role in helping mainstream schools develop their capacity for educating all pupils within their locality.

Bibliography

Ainscow, M. (1999) *Understanding the Development of Inclusive Schools*. London: Routledge Falmer Press.

Audit Commission (1992a) *Getting in on the Act: Provision for Pupils with Special Educational Needs: The National Perspective*. London: HMSO.

Audit Commission/HMI (1992b) *Getting the Act Together: A Management Handbook for Schools and Local Education Authorities*. London: HMSO.

Audit Commission/Ofsted (2001) *Managing Special Educational Needs: A Self-review Handbook for Local Education Authorities*. London: Audit Commission/Ofsted.

Audit Commission (2002) *Special Educational Needs: A Mainstream Issue*. London: HMSO.

Ballard, K. (1999) *Inclusive Education: International Voices on Disability and Justice*. London: Routledge Falmer Press.

Bangs J. (1993) 'Support services – stability or erosion?' *British Journal of Special Education*. **20** (3), 105–7.

Beek, C. (2002) *LEA and School Responsibilities within a Framework for Monitoring and Accountability*. Capita Strategic Education Services for the London Regional SEN Partnership (North Central Group).

Berg, I. (1997) 'Annotation: School refusal and truancy.' *Archives of Diseases in Childhood*, **76**, 90–1.

Berg, I. and Jackson, A. (1985). 'Teenage refusers grow up: a follow up study for 168 subjects 10 years on average after in-patient treatment'. *British Journal of Psychiatry*, **147**, 366–70.

Billington, T. (2002) *Separating, Losing and Excluding Children: Narratives of Difference*. London: RoutledgeFalmer Press.

Birmingham City Council Visiting Teacher Service (2002) *Pathways: A Profile to Record the Development and Progress of Young Children Who May Have Special Needs.* Birmingham City Council.

Blagg, N. and Yule, W. (1984) 'The behavioural treatment of school refusal – a comparative study'. *Behaviour Research and Therapy,* **22**, 119–27.

Bowers, T. (ed. 1991) *Schools, Services and Special Educational Needs: Management Issues in the Wake of LMS.* Perspective Press.

Clench, H. (2003) *Evaluating Education: Using the European Foundation for Quality Management Excellence Model.* South Central Regional Inclusion Project

DES (1988) *Circular 7/88 Education Reform Act; Local Management of Schools.* London: DES.

DfEE (1994) *Code of Practice on the Identification and Assessment of Special Educational Needs.* London: HMSO.

DfEE (1997) *Excellence for All Children: Meeting Special Educational Needs.* London: DfEE.

DfEE (1998) *Fair Funding: Improving Delegation to Schools: Consultation Paper.* London: HMSO.

DfES (1998) *Meeting Special Educational Needs: A Programme of Action.* London: HMSO.

DfES (2001a) *Revised Code of Practice on the Identification and Assessment of Special Educational Needs.* London: HMSO.

DfES (2001b) *Inclusive Schooling: Children with Special Educational Needs.* London: HMSO.

DfES (2001c) *Promoting Children's Mental Health within Early Years and Schools Settings.* London: HMSO.

DfES (2001d) *Guidance: Education of Young People in Public Care.* London: HMSO. www.dfes.gov.uk/incare/sections.shtml, issued alongside DoH (2000) Circular DH LAC (2000) 13. www.dfes.gov.uk/incare/Lac_2000_13.doc

DfES (2002) Education Protects Website. www.dfes.gov.uk/educationprotects

DfES (2003a) *Meeting Special Educational Needs: A Programme of Action.* London: HMSO.

DfES (2003b) *Code of Practice on Admissions.* http://www.dfes.gov.uk/sacode/main.shtml.

DfES (2003c) *Report of the Special Schools Working Group.*
http://www.dfes.gov.uk/consultations2/04/DfES-SSWG%20Summary.pdf

DfES/DoH (2001) *Access to Education for Children and Young People with Medical Needs.* DfES/DoH Ref DfES 0732/2001.

Department of Health (1989) *Introduction to the Children Act.* London: HMSO.

Department of Health (2002a) Quality Protects Website
www.doh.gov.uk/qualityprotects

Department of Health (2002b) *Outcome Indicators for Looked-After Children.* London: DoH. www.doh.gov.uk/public/oi2002.htm

Dessent, T. (1987) *Making the Ordinary School Special.* Lewes: Falmer Press.

Dessent, T. (1996) *Meeting SEN: Options for Partnership between Health, Education and Social Services.* Tamworth: NASEN.

Disability Rights Commission (2002) *Code of Practice for Schools.* Disability Rights Commission.

Duffield, J., Brown, S. and Riddell, S. (1995) 'The post Warnock learning support teacher: Where do specific learning difficulties fit in?' *Support for Learning* **1**:10, 22–8.

Elliott, J. G. (1999). 'Practitioner review: school refusal: Issues of conceptualisation, assessment and treatment'. *Journal of Child Psychology and Psychiatry* **40**:7, 1001–12.

Evans, R. and Docking, J. (1998) 'The impact of LEA policy on the role of the SENCO' in Davies, J. D. *et al. Managing Special Needs in Mainstream Schools.* London: David Fulton Publishers.

Evans, J. and Lunt, I. (1992) *Special Educational Needs under LMS.* London: Institute of Education Monograph.

Fever, F. (1994) *Who Cares?* New York: Time Warner.

Fletcher-Campbell, F. (1996) *The Resourcing of Special Educational Needs.* Slough: NFER.

Fletcher-Campbell, F. and Cullen, M. (1999) *The Impact of Delegation on LEA Support Services for Special Educational Needs.* Slough: NFER.

Garner, P. (1999) *Pupils with Problems: Rational Fears Radical Solutions.* London: Trentham Books.

Gilligan, R. (2001) *Promoting Resilience: A Resource Guide on Working with Children in the Care System.* London: British Association for Adoption and Fostering.

Gipps, C., Gross, H. and Goldstein, H. (1987) *Warnock's Eighteen Per Cent: Children with Special Needs in Primary Schools.* Lewes: Falmer Press.

Goodwin, C. (1983) 'The contribution of support services to integration policy' in Booth, T. and Potts, P. (eds) *Integrating Special Education.* Oxford: Blackwell.

Gowers, S. G., Harrington, R. C., Whitten, A. *et al.* (1998) *HoNSOSCA: Health of the Nation Outcome Scales for Children and Adolescents.* University of Liverpool.

Gray, P. J. (2001) *Developing Support for More Inclusive Schooling: A Review of the Role of Support Services for Special Educational Needs in English Local Authorities.* London: DfEE/NASEN.

Gray, P. J. (2002a) *How Good is Your Service? Regional Guidance on Evaluating Support Services for Children with Special Educational Needs.* East Midlands Special Educational Needs Regional Partnership.

Gray, P. J. (2002b) 'Custodians of entitlement or agents of dependence? SEN support services in the context of greater delegation of funding to schools'. *Support for Learning,* **17**(1), 5–8.

Gray, P. J., Miller, A. and Noakes, J. S. (1994) *Challenging Behaviour in Schools: Teacher Support, Practical Techniques and Policy Development.* London: Routledge.

Gross, J. (1996) 'The weight of parental evidence: parental advocacy and resource allocation to children with statements of special educational needs'. *Support for Learning,* **11**(1), 3–8.

Hart, S. (1997) *Beyond Special Needs: Enhancing Childrens' Learning Through Innovative Thinking.* London: Paul Chapman Publishing.

Hegarty, S., Pocklington, K. and Lucas, D. (1981) *Educating Pupils with Special Needs in the Ordinary School.* Windsor: NFER Nelson.

HMI (Scotland) (2002) *Count Us In: Achieving Inclusion in Scottish Schools..* Edinburgh: HMSO. www.scotland.gov.uk/hmie

HMSO (1995) Disablility Discrimination Act 1995. London: HMSO.

HMSO (2001) *Special Educational Needs and Disability Act.* London: HMSO. http://www.hmso.gov.uk/acts/acts2001/20010010.htm

HMSO (2003) *The Children at Risk.* Green Paper. London: HMSO.

House of Commons Education Committee (1993) Third Report of 92/3 Session: HC 287. London: HMSO.

Inclusive Education Review Group (2002) *A Systematic Review of the Effectiveness of School-level Actions for Promoting Participation by All Students.* http://eppi.ioe.ac.uk/EPPIWeb/home.aspx?page=/reel/review_groups/inclusion/review_one.htm

Jackson, S. and Sachdev, D. (2001) *Better Education, Better Futures*. London: Barnados.

Jackson, S., Ajayi, S. and Quigle, M. (2003) *By Degrees: The First Year*. London: Frank Buttle Trust.

Katzenbach, J. and Smith, D. (1993) *The Wisdom of Teams: Creating High Performance Organisation*. Boston: Harvard Business School.

Kearney, C. A. and Beasley, J. F. (1994) 'The clinical treatment of school refusal behaviour: a survey of referral and practice characteristics'. *Psychology in Schools* **31**, 128–32.

Kearney, C. A. and Silverman, W. K. (1990) 'Family environment of youngsters with school refusal behaviour: a synopsis with implications for assessment and treatment.' *American Journal of Family Therapy*, **23** 59–72.

Kelly, G. (1955) *The Psychology of Personal Constructs*. New York: Norton.

Kent CC (2000) *All Together Better*. Kent County Council.

Kent CC (2001) *Local Learning Groups Toolkit*. Kent County Council.

Kent CC (2002) *Best Value Review of School Improvement Services in Kent*. Kent County Council.

King, N. and Ollendick, T. H. (1997). 'Treatment of Child Phobias'. *Journal of Child Psychology and Psychiatry*, **28**, 389–400.

Knight, R. (1993) *Special Educational Needs and the Application of Resources*. Slough: EMIE.

Lacey, P. (2001) *Support Partnerships: Collaboration in Action*. London: David Fulton Publishers.

Lacey, P. and Lomas, J. (1993) *Support Services and the Curriculum: A Practical Guide to Collaboration*. London: David Fulton Publishers.

Last, C. G., Hansen, C. and Franco, N. (1998) 'Cognitive-behavioural treatment of school phobia'. *Journal of the American Academy of Child and Adolescent Psychiatry*, **37**(4), 404–11.

Leathard, A. (ed.) (1994) *Going Interprofessional: Working Together for Health and Welfare*. London: Routledge.

Lee, T., (1992) 'Local management of schools and special education' in Booth, T., Swan, W., Masterton, M. and Potts, P. (eds) *Learning for All. Policy for Diversity in Education*. London: Routledge.

Lindsey, G. (2000) 'Summary of Discussion' in Norwich, B. (ed.) *Specialist Teaching for Special Educational Needs and Inclusion*. Tamworth: NASEN.

Lindsey, G. (2003) 'Inclusive education: a critical perspective.' *British Journal of Special Education*. **30** (1), NASEN.

Locke, A. and Beech, M. (1991) *Teaching Talking Profiles.* Reading: NFER-Nelson.

Marsh, A. (1998) 'Resourcing inclusive education: the real economics' in Clough, P. (ed.) *Managing Inclusive Education.* London: Paul Chapman Publishing.

Masi, G. Mucci, M. and Millepiedi, S. (2001) 'Separation anxiety disorder in children and adolescents: epidemiology, diagnosis and management'. *CNS,* **15**(2), 93–104.

McLaughlin, C. (1989) 'Working face to face: aspects of interpersonal work' *Support for Learning* **4**(2), 96–101.

Meltzer, H. and Gatward, R. (2000) *Mental Health of Children and Adolescents in Great Britain.* London: The Stationery Office.

Mental Health Foundation (1999) *Bright Futures: Promoting Children and Young People's Mental Health.* London: The Mental Health Foundation.

Millar, S. (1995) *Use of Personal Passports with Deafblind People* (Final report). Scottish Office Education Department Funded Project. Scotland: SENSE.

Moore, J. and Morrison, N. (1988) *Someone Else's Problem: Teacher Development to Meet Special Educational Needs.* Lewes: Falmer Press.

Morris, J. (2002) *A Lot to Say.* London: Scope.

Moses, D., Hegarty, S. and Jowett, S. (1988) *Supporting Ordinary Schools.* Windsor: NFER-Nelson.

NASEN (1999): *Position Statement on Delegation of SEN Support Services to Schools,* 23rd November 1999. Tamworth: NASEN.

NCC (1989) *A Curriculum for All* (Curriculum Guidance 2) London: National Curriculum Council.

Ofsted (2001) *Evaluating Educational Inclusion.* London: Ofsted.

Ofsted and Audit Commission (2002) *Local Education Authorities and School Improvement 1996–2001.* London: Audit Commission.

Orlove, F. and Sobsey, D. (1991) *Educating Children with Multiple Disabilities: A Transdisciplinary Approach.* Baltimore: Paul Brookes.

Parsons, C. (1997) *Report of the Survey of English LEAs on Permanent Exclusions from Schools 1996–7.* Canterbury: Christ Church University College.

Perugi, G., Deltito, J., Soriam, A. *et al.* (1988) 'Relationships between panic disorder and separation anxiety with school phobia'. *Comprehensive Psychiatry,* **29**, 98–107.

QCA (2000) *Inclusion Statement.* http://www.nc.uk.net/inclusion.htm

Reger, R. (1972) 'The medical model in special education'. *Psychology in Schools* **9** pp 8–12.

Rees, G. (2001) *Working with Young Runaways.* London: The Children's Society.

Roaf, C. (2002) *Co-ordinating Services for Included Children.* Buckingham: Open University Press.

RNID/University of Hertfordshire (2002) *Inclusion: What Deaf Pupils Think.* London: RNID.

Scottish Council for Educational Technology (2002) Pioneer Virtual Learning Environment. http://www.itscotland.com/services/pioneer.asp

Scottish Executive (2001) *Learning with Care.* Scotland: HMSO. http://www.scotland.gov.uk/library3/education/lacr.pdf

Social Exclusion Unit (2002) *Young Runaways.* London: Office of the Deputy Prime Minister.

Social Exclusion Unit (2003) *A Better Education for Children in Care.* London: Office of the Deputy Prime Minister.

Statutory instrument no. 478 (2000) *The Financing of Maintained Schools (England) Regulations.* London: HMSO.

Tansey, K. (1995) 'This can't be my responsibility: it must be yours! An analysis of a reintegration programme for a school refuser'. *British Journal of Special Education,* **22**, 12–15.

Teacher Training Agency (1999) *National Special Educational Needs Specialist Standards.* London: TTA.

Thomas, G. (1992) *Effective Classroom Teamwork: Support or Intrusion?* London: Routledge.

Thomas, G., Walker, D. and Webb, J. (1998) *The Making of the Inclusive School.* London: Routledge.

Tomlinson, S. (1982) *A Sociology of Special Education.* Routledge and Kegan Paul: Henley on Thames.

UNESCO (1994) *The Salamanca Statement.* Paris: UNESCO.

The Who Cares? Trust (1998) *Remember My Messages.* London: The Who Cares? Trust.

The Who Cares? Trust (2003) *Education Matters.* London: The Who Cares? Trust.

Welsh Assembly (2001) *Children First.* Wales: HMSO. http://www.childrenfirst.wales.gov.uk/content/about.htm

Index

Bold indicates main mentions. *Italic* indicates figures and tables not included in the text page range.